NEGOTIATING
OFFICE
SPACE

T0117575

NEGOTIATING OFFICE SPACE

What Business Owners Need to Know Before Signing on the Dotted Line

Robert Miller, CCIM

Advantage®

Published by Advantage, Charleston, South Carolina.
Member of Advantage Media Group.

ADVANTAGE is a registered trademark and the Advantage colophon is a trademark of Advantage Media Group, Inc.

Printed in the United States of America.

ISBN: 978-1-59932-201-8
LCCN: 2010905069

This publication is designed to provide accurate and authoritative information in regard to the subject matter covered. It is sold with the understanding that the publisher is not engaged in rendering legal, accounting, or other professional services. If legal advice or other expert assistance is required, the services of a competent professional person should be sought.

Most Advantage Media Group titles are available at special quantity discounts for bulk purchases for sales promotions, premiums, fundraising, and educational use. Special versions or book excerpts can also be created to fit specific needs.

For more information, please write: Special Markets, Advantage Media Group, P.O. Box 272, Charleston, SC 29402 or call 1.866.775.1696.

Visit us online at **advantagefamily**.com

Table of Contents

CHAPTER 1   11
The 5 Stages of Commercial
Office Leasing

CHAPTER 2   15
The Leasing Time Line

CHAPTER 3   23
Establish Your Budget

CHAPTER 4   25
Determine Your Space Requirements

CHAPTER 5   29
Identify Where Employees Live

CHAPTER 6   31
Corporate Image and Growth – What Sort of Image Do You Want Your Space to Portray?

CHAPTER 7   33
Gather Market Data

CHAPTER 8   35
The Broker Game

CHAPTER 9   39
11 Questions You Must Ask Before Hiring A Broker

CHAPTER 10   47
Pre-Screening and Selecting Properties to Visit

CHAPTER 11   51
Understanding Rental Rates

CHAPTER 12   55
How Space Is Measured

CHAPTER 13   57
Space Configuration Effects Efficiency

CHAPTER 14   61
Touring Properties

CHAPTER 15   65
Questions You Might Be Asked

CHAPTER 16   69
The Letter-of-Intent Proposal

CHAPTER 17   81
Lease Negotiations to Lease Execution

CHAPTER 18   85
Common Lease Clauses

CHAPTER 19   99
14 Negotiating Tips for Your Counter Offer

CHAPTER 20   105
Negotiating Strategies

CHAPTER 21   113
7 Critical Negotiating Techniques

CHAPTER 22   121
Renewing or Extending a Lease

CHAPTER 23   125
Lease Execution

CHAPTER 24   129
Take Control of the Construction Process

CHAPTER 25   135
Construction Begins

CHAPTER 26   139
Vendor Coordination

CHAPTER 27   141
The Final Walk-Thru: It's Moving Day

CHAPTER 28   143
Congratulations– You're Home

Appendix   146

**Glossary of Common
Leasing Terms**   147

FREE Lease Proposal
Evaluation Consultation   160

What is the Platinum
Office Leasing Program?   161

Introduction

The adage that any process is a marathon and not a sprint is never more true than in the leasing of commercial office space. Too often, Tenants wait until the very last minute to make a decision about their space and then are forced to rush through many potential spaces with too little time for proper space or lease considerations. The result gives the Tenant a space that is acceptable but not necessarily what he wants and with terms that are again acceptable but are not written in the best interest of the Tenant. The Tenant may have gotten what he needed but not what he wanted and that is a world of difference!

This book is written from the perspective of a Tenant having the advantage of time. Time to incorporate the business planning, to review and hire the most qualified real estate broker, to find the appropriate space, to negotiate the lease terms and time to complete any necessary remodeling. The best way to do this is for the Tenant to schedule time wisely and organize a time line.

In considering what would be the best avenue for the Tenant to follow in order to get these simple, yet time consuming tasks accomplished, we have developed a winning timeline that provides a guide to follow. The timeline depicts what steps to take in the process of leasing office space and, if not more importantly, when to begin each activity so that there is a comfortable amount of time to do all of the tasks required in timing your office lease.

This book will also provide you with the tools that will be vital to your success. This book is not just a how to guide but provides the forms and instructions that have been tested by many of our clients and have been shown to give them the edge in leasing their office spaces.

About the Author

ROBERT A. MILLER, CCIM, RPA

 Robert is the Founder and President of the Miller Group LLC a Specialized Office Leasing Firm providing Leasing Information and Consulting Services to Atlanta Property Owners. Robert first formed The Miller Group LLC to provide Leasing and Management services for office buildings that he owned with several partners.

"We simply were not happy with the quality and attention that we were getting from other companies. Agents weren't interested in aggressively pursuing leads for the small office spaces that we had vacant." Being more motivated as an owner than as a broker making fees, Robert took over the leasing and management and marketed aggressively to fill the vacancies.

After seeing the results of Robert's attention to detail, numerous friends and business associates ask him to fill the vacancies in their office buildings. Having been on all sides of the real estate table, Robert brings a unique set of skills to office leasing and property management which allow him to successfully network and bring together all parties to ensure a successful transaction.

Robert possesses over 20 years of experience in real estate development, construction management, office leasing and property management. Over the five years, Robert has negotiated office leases representing three million square feet and $10 million in value. He has been involved in the acquisition and sale of office, industrial and retail properties. He also represents a wide variety of small business owners including doctors, dentist, chiropractors, attorneys, insurance and financial planners. Having worked on both sides of the table, representing landlord and tenants, Robert understands the needs of all parties which make him uniquely qualified to find the creative solutions which allow everyone to walk away from the negotiations a winner.

Robert is a graduate of Purdue University with a Bachelor's degree in Construction Management and holds a Master of Science in Real Estate from Georgia State University. He has been designated a Certified Commercial Investment Member (CCIM), a designation held by only 4% of all commercial real estate practitioners, and Real Property Administrator (RPA), the designation awarded property managers who have demonstrated excellence and experience in real estate management in both the classroom and business world.

As President of The Miller Group, LLC, Robert oversees daily operations of the Property Management and Landlord Leasing division consisting of approximately 405 tenants and 750,000 square feet of commercial office buildings. He is directly responsible for marketing, leasing, budgeting, investor reporting, staffing, and policy and procedure implementation.

Robert resides in Dunwoody, Georgia with his wife Meri and his three daughters: Summer, Katie and Abigail.

CHAPTER 1

The 5 Stages of Commercial Office Leasing

You are about to embark on one of the most important aspects of your business' existence, locating an office space. Whether it means finding a new lease or renewing an existing lease, your office space will have a major impact on the success or failure of your business. According to national surveys, leasing and office space costs are companies' second highest expenses, right behind salaries and employee benefits. In fact, for many small to midsize companies, this will be the highest fixed monthly expenditure. Not only can the leasing decision determine economic gains, but it can also provide for the welfare of your employees as well as your clients. The key to all of this is using the time that is required to ensure success in this endeavor. It is imperative that a prospective Tenant begins the space review process early, allowing for careful consideration of all aspects demanded in each step of the lease process. This book is written to incorporate a 7 month window prior to the end of your existing lease agreement. This strategy will ensure that the process of planning, hiring, finding, negotiating, implementing and relocation gives the Tenant the best opportunity for success. By planning well in advance, time will be your ally, not your enemy.

If your intent is to renew the lease at your existing location it is critical that you start the process early. The only way to get the best deal is to follow the same process as if you were moving.

If time becomes an issue, keep cool, because most economic concessions are made right before the deadline of a transaction. Avoid telegraphing your need to close the deal quickly. Attempt to work out alternative solutions with your existing landlord rather than reveal that you are under time pressure.

Allow enough time to accomplish all of your objectives by following the time line of the leasing process. Here is a quick overview of the process. Based upon how much time you actually have to accomplish your move, you may have to compress the time frames suggested.

There are five essential and distinct stages of the commercial office leasing process. Although they are separate functions, when coordinated with the leasing timeline they will provide an effective and efficient transaction process that, in the end, will provide your business the optimal return on the time invested. That is you can expect the right space for the right price and term. These stages are:

6-7 Months Away	Planning Stage
5-4 Months Away	Market Research
4-3 Months Away	Property Review
3-2 Months Away	Proposal/Negotiation
2-1 Months Away	Design & Construction

The efforts made to strictly adhere to the requirements associated with each of these stages will culminate in an easy move into your new space. It is important to note that much of the information depicted in these stages can also be applicable to those companies in the process of renewing their lease. As with a new lease, the information contained will give the Tenant the ability to negotiate with the Landlord from a position of strength as opposed to just accepting the terms of the landlord's offer. Regardless of which position your business may be in, adhering to the timeline will afford the user the greatest opportunity to get the deal they need for the terms they want.

## CHAPTER 2

The Leasing Time Line

After years of negotiating commercial office leases, we've found that businesses who were the most successful in their leasing transactions, followed this timeline.

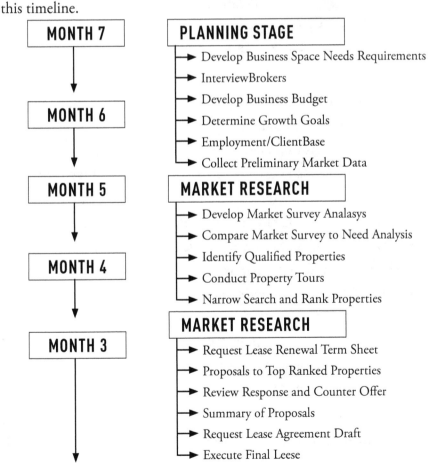

MONTH 7	**PLANNING STAGE**
	→ Develop Business Space Needs Requirements
	→ InterviewBrokers
	→ Develop Business Budget
MONTH 6	→ Determine Growth Goals
	→ Employment/ClientBase
	→ Collect Preliminary Market Data
MONTH 5	**MARKET RESEARCH**
	→ Develop Market Survey Analasys
	→ Compare Market Survey to Need Analysis
	→ Identify Qualified Properties
MONTH 4	→ Conduct Property Tours
	→ Narrow Search and Rank Properties
	MARKET RESEARCH
MONTH 3	→ Request Lease Renewal Term Sheet
	→ Proposals to Top Ranked Properties
	→ Review Response and Counter Offer
	→ Summary of Proposals
	→ Request Lease Agreement Draft
	→ Execute Final Leese

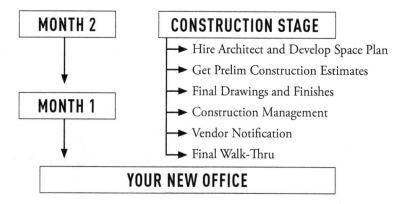

It's not enough to show a time line without giving an overview of its individual aspects:

PLANNING STAGE

Seven to Five Months before Anticipated
Lease Commencement or Renewal

Develop a complete plan of your businesses requirements, wants and goals. This time will encompass meeting with all of your managers and department heads, considering space needs, developing economic or budgeting constraints, determining growth goals and marrying them to your company's strategic plans. Deciding on potential geographic areas that suit your employees and/or your client base, and acquiring as much market, building rate and term information as you can is critical. If you are planning to hire an experienced office broker, he will supply much of the market information you will need, which will save you a considerable amount of time and energy.

MARKET RESEARCH

Five to Four Months before Anticipated
Lease Commencement or Renewal

Begin to survey the market and locate available properties that meet your requirements. Compare the market survey to your needs analysis. Conduct inspection tours of the most qualified properties and begin the process of narrowing the number of spaces that match your corporate goals.

PROPERTY REVIEW
Four to Three Months before Anticipated Lease Commencement or Renewal

Develop negotiating strategy for top ranked property. If your intent is to remain in your existing space, send a renewal term sheet to the present Landlord. Begin making preliminary proposals and open negotiations on the properties that match your corporate goals.

PROPOSAL/NEGOTIATION STAGE
Three to Two Months before Anticipated Lease Commencement or Renewal

Begin reviewing responses and evaluate the counter offers. Negotiate strategically and without fear until consensus is reached on the economic terms of the offers. Select the offer that best matches your company goals and desires that were determined during the planning stage. Once an economic agreement is reached, a review of the actual lease contract can begin. This process can typically take two or more weeks for review of the legal documentation. Commence the preliminary space planning process to determine best-fit suitability. If you are permitted to hire an architect, now is the time to complete that process. Often times the Landlord will supply the space planning service as part of their Tenant Improvement allowance. Cost estimates can take up to another two weeks. Review space plans, and cost estimates. Lease contract negotiations should take place. If all has gone smoothly you may find yourself at the point of signing a lease.

CONSTRUCTION STAGE

Final Two Months before Anticipated Lease Commencement or Renewal

The construction period. Working drawings for your tenant improvements are complete, based upon previous meetings regarding your space plan. Work will begin after lease execution. Allow two to three weeks for these plans to be completed. Permits (where and when required) can take from 2 to 6 weeks depending on the various approvals required. Most landlords will commence improvement construction upon application for permits to expedite the occupancy. Depending on the size of the job you should allow 8 to 12 weeks for the physical construction.

You will also begin the process of vendor notification of the new office space. This will include getting phone and data service aligned with any construction project, ordering new stationery, acquiring furniture, locating and scheduling the moving company and any other jobs that are necessary for your specialized company needs.

FINAL CHECK LIST

One Month before Anticipated Lease Commencement or Renewal

Review and re-review the construction process. Also make sure that the tasks and jobs related to the move itself are confirmed so that by the time commencement begins, everything you desire for a smooth transition is done.

As you can see, the lease process time line has numerous components that, when implemented effectively, can require 20-26 weeks for a smooth and cost effective relocation. If in the event you are short on time, there are some short cuts to compress the time required, but they can cost your business money and negotiating power. A solution to this scenario may be to limit your choices to buildings with space that comes very close to your needs and making only minor alterations, or looking for sublease space meeting your requirements. Regardless of what path you select, whenever possible, it is imperative to give yourself the opportunity to be successful in your next lease transaction. Start the process by allowing yourself the maximum amount of time for gathering the necessary information for you to make the best decisions.

STAGE I

6-7 MONTHS AWAY: Planning Stage

There are several elements of planning that must be considered, dealt with and completed before determining what actions to take in the office leasing process. Although some of this may be obvious, it is good to reiterate the importance of planning as many elements are often overlooked during the leasing process.

CHAPTER 3

Establish Your Budget

I t is amazing to me how many successful business people running multi-million (if not billion) dollar companies begin the process of finding new office space without knowing what they can afford to spend. Considering that this expense is, for many businesses, the second largest expense a company may have next to salaries, it is paramount that the person responsible for choosing office space both understand and is comfortable with the company's rent expense exposure. It is important to know your price range before looking at office space to eliminate wasting time and money reviewing spaces that you just can't afford.

Unfortunately, there is no exact science or formula to get a defined answer to this. If I were to arbitrarily say that your rent budget should be 20% of your annual overall expense budget it would be a disservice to small and large companies alike. A large law firm, in many cases, may have the revenue stream to support a rent payment that is much higher than a non-profit organization. If we were to use this 20% rule here, it may be a deal for the law firm but a burden for the non-profit company.

The key in most cases is to not get emotional about the office space. Remember, this is a business decision...one that could have a major impact on the success or failure of your company. Do the math! Make sure that you know what your business can afford today and not what may put you out of business tomorrow.

CHAPTER 4

Determine Your Space Requirements

There are a number of important questions to ask to accurately define your requirements. Doing this in advance will save you time and avoid starting in the wrong direction. Committing your requirements to paper will also help you as you visit properties to make sure that nothing is overlooked. As a broker, there are a number of questions I ask my clients to move from a rough idea of their needs to a clearly defined objective. You will use this information to screen out unsuitable properties once you start to make calls on available sites. The Space Needs Worksheet (found in the appendix) highlights the following issues:

- Number of private offices

- Sizes: Executive_____ Associate_____ Sales_____

- Number of open area work-stations: Sizes: 6x6   8x8   8x10 other

- Number of conference rooms and sizes

- Number of storage/supply rooms and sizes

- Number or size of computer room

- How large a reception area is required?

- Do you have any special electrical requirements?

- Other special requirements?

- Electrical needs

- Communication needs

- Special HVAC (heating, ventilating and air conditioning) needs

Generally you will have some idea of how much space you will need based upon your prior experience, research of competing businesses, or franchiser provided guidelines. Deciding how many square feet you will need is the next step in starting your search for space. As a rule of thumb, for office users, plan on between 150 to 200 square feet per person. To get a more accurate feel for your square footage requirements, use the chart below to calculate your needs. Select your anticipated square foot usage from the range given for each use and multiply it by the number of people needing that configuration. Generally, leases run from three to five years so remember to anticipate personnel growth in your calculations. After you have completed the math for all your uses; add 30% to the total to compute the circulation for corridors and the load factor.

Use	Usable Sq. Ft. per person	Estimated Size	Number of People	Total Sq. Ft. Required
Sr. Executive	250-400	X	=	
Executive	150-250	X	=	
Private Office	100-150	X	=	
Partitioned/Open	50-100	X	=	
Conference Rooms	25-30	X	=	
Reception Room	100+25/guest	X	=	
Kitchen/Lounge	50+15/person	X	=	
File Room	7 per file	X	=	
Subtotal				
Circulation/Load Factor	Add 30% Subtotal			
			Total Required	

CHAPTER 5

Identify Where Employees Live

M ore often than not, the top executive of a business may desire to locate the office near where he lives as opposed to either where the majority of his employees live or where the best qualified employees could come from. This is why often an executive doesn't understand why his employees get into the office late, leave early and do not get the overall production expected. Since employees generally can't afford to live near the boss they face long commutes and traffic getting to the office. By taking the time to complete an inventory of where your employees live, you may develop a better understanding of where to locate your office. By identifying a common zip code among the employees you may determine an area that better suits the production needs of the company.

IDENTIFY WHERE YOUR CLIENT BASE COMES FROM.

Many businesses exist to be convenient to the clients they serve. This is not just restricted to retail types of companies any more. Service professionals like doctors, dentists, CPA's and lawyers are taking a closer look at the location demographics of their client base. That is why it is important for businesses to know where their clients live and/or work in order to better serve their needs and ultimately gain greater market share. Developing customer tracking systems and databases can make this easier. If you are a new company determining demographics on the ideal customer will give you a reference point with which to compare different possible locations. Uncovering demographic data from public resources or from a competent real estate broker will help you in this area as well.

CHAPTER 6

Corporate Image and Growth - What Sort of Image Do You Want Your Space to Portray?

Different businesses have different space image and type requirements. You wouldn't expect to see a law firm interior/image in a doctor's office. Determine the type of image that is important to your firm. Some important issues that require resolution include:

- What particular buildings are of interest?
- Is an office with a view important?
- What is the lowest floor your company would be willing to occupy?
- What in building amenities are important?
- What near building amenities are important?
- What level of finish are you willing to accept?
- What are your parking and transportation needs?

Incorporate your business' strategic growth plans into this process.

Imagine moving into an office space that is ideal for your company today yet two years into the lease you are busting at the seams because the growth that you had planned on actually came to fruition. Unfortunately, you have three years left on the lease and you still have more growth plans. Make sure that you apply your strategic plans into the conversation regarding your space needs. This doesn't mean that you need to get all of the space today, much less pay for it, but you should be prepared to create an action plan with the existing space when such growth should occur.

CHAPTER 7

Gather Market Data

Acquire the market data information for the areas you need to be in. Your knowledge of the market will substantially increase the level of success you will have with the next lease transaction you are about to embark on. You have undoubtedly heard the phrase "why would you get into a gun fight without a gun?!" Well, the same idea applies here. You need to have a working knowledge of rents, vacancies, products, concessions and locations in order to level the playing field in the lease negotiation. The Internet will be a great resource to help you gather the market information that you will need. There are a number of great searchable web sites you can access and most of them will come up on a search with some common key words such as office space, industrial space and retail space. Some useful sites include:

- www.costar.com

- www.blacksguide.com

- www.tmgleasing.com

- www.globeSt.com

- www.ccimnet.com

- www.loopnet.com

These sites will be a good place to start. I suggest you go on line and get familiar with how these sites work.

You will want to check the classified ads in the local and business newspapers and drive around the areas you consider suitable for your business. The best time to drive the market is early Sunday morning. There is no traffic so it's easy to pull over and capture an address and phone number. I suggest a small tape or digital recorder for this job. Not only is it faster and easier, but also it will allow you to record a few comments about the building and its location. This will be useful later when you make your screening calls. Using a digital camera with voice recording capacity will definitely save you time and effort when deciding which properties you will want to visit. Hiring a specialized office leasing broker will save you a lot of time and shoe leather during this data collection stage and will provide the most up to date information.

CHAPTER 8

The Broker Game

Using a qualified commercial office broker will save you time and money. Not only will your broker do much of the grunt work involved in the leasing process, he will also have a deeper market knowledge and better market information. By using this guide, you will be better able to manage your broker and your transaction. You will have a better understanding of the process and know what to expect. This will put you in control of your transaction and, since you are the one who lives with the lease, control is exactly what you need.

As you start the process of finding office space you will encounter commercial brokers, some of whom will offer their services to you. It is vital that you are clear on whom the broker is representing in your transaction. The broker representing the Landlord is called the "Landlord Rep" and the broker representing you is the "Tenant Rep". A dual agency is when a broker represents both parties simultaneously in a transaction. You will want a broker working on your behalf; you will want a "Tenant Rep". The broker is generally paid by the landlord so there is usually no cost to you for retaining your own broker.

Real estate brokers are either specialists or generalists. In leasing you need to be working with a specialist if you are using a broker. Commercial leasing brokers generally fall into two categories: full service brokers who can serve as agents for both landlords and tenants; and tenant only representatives ("tenant rep"). The last is a minority in today's market as most brokers offer full service assistance.

You are also likely to encounter the in-house building representative who is not an agent of the owner but is an employee. Employees do not have a fiduciary duty to any party on the transaction, often are not real estate licensees and act in the best interest of their employer. When encountering anyone representing a property of interest to you, be sure to ask if they are an agent or an employee of the owner.

It is likely that if you interview several brokers before beginning your search for new space, you will encounter both the full service broker and the tenant rep broker. The key to selecting any broker is experience. Often the tenant rep's strongest selling point is that, because they represent you, they can get you the best deal. A thorough understanding of how "agency" affects lease negotiations will clarify this statement.

The source of an agent's compensation, if any, does not solely determine agency. Agency is an action. That is, if a real estate licensee acts as someone's agent, they become their agent. A broker owes their principal a fiduciary duty or, in other words an absolutely faithful duty to perform in the best interest of their principal and to do no harm. They also have a duty of honest and fair dealing with all other parties in the transaction.

Whether a broker works for a full service brokerage or a tenant representation brokerage, the agent's fiduciary duty is always to their principal. That is why experience is the most important factor in selecting a broker. In evaluating experience, consider both the depth and the volume of experience. A full service broker, because he often represents several local properties, receives as well as initiates transactions. The full service broker develops strong problem solving and negotiating skills because they are experienced with both sides of transactions.

If you plan on using a broker, I suggest you select a qualified specialist in the area and type of property you desire. To ensure that you have the dedicated attention of your agent and their commitment to serve you and stay with you until you have completed your lease transaction you will want to get an exclusive representation agreement. This agreement will detail the duties and tasks that everyone will be required to fulfill in order to have a successful transaction. You need to put your agreement in writing and include the right to terminate the agreement on five to ten days written notice. In this way you can end the relationship quickly if your broker is not doing an outstanding job for you. Brokers are very useful and can save your time and effort and that translates into money.

There are very specific questions you should ask a potential broker to insure that you get the best representation for your needs. Many Brokers would prefer that you don't even ask these questions because the knowledge you will gain from their honest answers will give you a very good idea of what outcome you can expect from using this Broker and, let's face it, in real estate as in life all things are NOT created equal.

CHAPTER 9

11 Questions You Must Ask Before Hiring A Broker

Hiring a real estate Broker is just like any hiring process with you on the boss's side of the desk. It is critical that you make the right decision about who will handle one of the more critical financial decisions you will make. Whether you decide to lease your next office space on your own or hire a professional to handle it for you, there are certain key facts that can literally cost or save you thousands of dollars.

"DO YOU SPECIALIZE IN LEASING OFFICE PROPERTIES?"

So many commercial real estate brokers have no specialty at all. They will show a warehouse on Monday, try to sell a gas station on Wednesday and want to show you OFFICE SPACE on Friday. The best brokers for leasing office space are specialist in Office Leasing. Because of this they will have a thorough knowledge of all the buildings in their markets as well as experience with many different office lease formats and new structures. A lack of knowledge and commitment to a specialty will cost you time and money in the finding of your new office space. Prior to working with a broker be sure to ask how many offices leases he has performed and the savings he has made his clients. Finally, get and review references.

"WHAT CAN YOU TELL ME ABOUT YOUR KNOWLEDGE OF THE MARKET?"

Nothing will cost you more than using a Broker that does not know what is happening in the marketplace that they are supposed to serve. Uncovering what the prospective Tenant Broker knows about Market Rates, Vacancies, Improvement and Concession trends can be the difference between costing and saving you thousands on your next lease. If the Broker doesn't know the answers to theses questions, you don't want to know them.

"HOW LONG HAVE YOU BEEN BROKERING TENANTS IN THIS MARKET?"

Not unlike the "jack-of-all-trades" question above, it is important to know the Brokers level of experience level and knowledge of the area you want to locate your business. A Broker should not only know the different buildings in the market but, also the Brokers and Landlords through established relationships. This will save you thousands in Leasing costs as your Broker will know what the Landlord can do as opposed to what has been put forth on the surface.

"WHAT RESOURCES WILL THE BROKERS USE TO HELP THEM FIND YOUR NEXT OFFICE SPACE?"

If your Broker is relying solely on the Sunday paper and/or drive-bys for the most up to date information on available space, he is wasting his time and, probably, your money. A good Broker will subscribe to a listing service, such as CoStar, Doreys, CEIX, that will provide at least 97% of all current and accurate available space, lease, vacancy, improvement and rate history information available. This knowledge is vital to your success in identifying the right space for the right deal.

"WHAT DEALS HAVE YOU BEEN INVOLVED IN LATELY?"

It may seem like everywhere you look many commercial real estate Brokers are boasting about being "Number One" for this or that or quote you the number of clients that they have represented (it seems that Coca Cola is a client of everyone) or they are a member of the Million Dollar Club (that club is not for brokers that have SAVED tenants a MILLION Dollars). If you are like many office space renters, you probably have become immune to much of this information. After all, what should you care how much money a broker made last year! The only thing you really care about is whether they can find the right space for you and save you MONEY!!

Ask your Broker about the type of deals he has recently completed or is working on. The answer to this question may eliminate him from consideration. In fact, he may have no answer at all. You need to know if the broker is innovative in his approach to deal making or does he simply stay in the preverbal "box." A Broker who is a problem solver can create non-traditional ways to get a difficult deal done. In most instances, that means saving you money on rent or the flexibility in terms you need.

"WHAT TYPE OF ASSISTANCE DO YOU HAVE TO HELP FIND MY SPACE?"

Most Brokers work all by themselves or pair up with another single Broker, making it very difficult for them to provide you with a consistent, superior level of service. The job of real estate has many varied parts to it. Just as you wouldn't expect a doctor or a lawyer to answer phones or type letters, your real estate Broker shouldn't be spending his or her time on simple but time-consuming tasks that could be delegated. If this Broker does not have assistance to cover the areas mentioned, you should ask yourself how much time does he really have to find your next office space?

"CAN YOU PROVIDE ME WITH A COMPLETE LIST OF REFERENCES ON THE DEALS YOU HAVE DONE?"

Although this may be common sense, it is amazing how many company leaders hire Brokers based solely on a brief meeting, a pretty brochure, a sharp suit and a handshake. Demand and, at least, spot check references to get a sense of the Brokers ability to perform in good and bad times. The 10 minutes you spend here can save you thousand of dollars when it comes time for your Broker to negotiate the deal.

"WHAT OFFICE INNOVATIONS OR TRENDS DO YOU SEE COMING AHEAD?"

Asking your Broker what he sees ahead in the market place could mean the difference between finding 10,000 square feet of inefficient space that may be on the block today while actually needing only 6,000 square feet in a better designed building coming up down the street. Also, knowledge about creative lease methods and terms, as well as tax changes and its potential effect on your lease, will have a bottom line effect on your balance sheet.

"WHERE DO YOU RANK WITHIN YOUR COMPANY?"

Within a company every Broker will have the same resources and opportunities. How well a broker will thrive on this level playing field will give you further indication of how successfully he will be finding your next office space.

"HOW MANY COMPANIES LIKE MY FIRM HAVE YOU WORKED OR ARE YOU WORKING WITH?"

Obviously, the more similar clients your Broker is working with, the greater the probability that he knows your business and already has an idea of the type of project that will suit you for the terms that are available and appropriate.

"WHAT VALUE DO YOU BRING TO MY COMPANY?"

It is a much tougher real estate market than it used to be. Finding a Broker who has the tenacity to get the deal done and to go beyond what you would expect him to will literally make you money. If they can't answer this question, then you should thank them and send them on their way. If not even refer them to your competitor.

When it is all said and done, a qualified real estate broker will provide the expertise that will help you acquire and analyze the data in whatever shape or format you need. Moreover, the broker will allow you to do what you do best…run your business while they do what they do best…that is making office leasing deals. The trick to finding a qualified broker, the expert if you will, is to do the work and ask the questions…the questions that will make most brokers nervous, but will get you the broker that will serve your needs and not his own.

STAGE II

4-5 MONTHS AWAY: Market Research

Now you are ready to begin the process of reviewing office buildings. If you have made the decision to hire a qualified broker, this will be much easier because the broker will do much of the work for you and provide you the most up to date information and expertise available. If you are going it alone, then there are several key issues that you need to be aware of prior to beginning the search.

CHAPTER 10

Pre-Screening and Selecting Properties to Visit

Now you are ready to get the information to make your next transaction a success. But where do you start? The first thing you must do is know the markets that you want to locate your office in. You've made some planning decisions and are ready to get the information that will help you make the best use of your time in viewing, proposing, negotiating and constructing your next office space. Without this information, you will not be in a position of strength when it comes time to do the remaining functions in the leasing process.

What type of questions or issues do you need to be aware of? To answer this question, let me give you some strategies to help you understand and narrow your search in order to save you time and money:

Get market rental information from all the landlords that you think you are interested in. This will usually come in the form of a flyer and can provide you with the pertinent information that will help you eliminate projects which:

- don't match your budget considerations

- don't immediately offer enough tenant improvement allowances

- don't have a lease structure that suits your requirements

Get Existing Space Plans from the properties/projects you believe fit your planning goals before you ever leave your office. Why get in your car, travel X number of miles to go to numerous office spaces that, although the square footage measurement met your needs, the space does not meet your planning goals. Some web sites you will use to find space will have plans posted. You can also ask the landlord to fax or e-mail plans to you. Email is better for this purpose because it provides a better package, usually in color. Since your outcome is to save time and effort, be prepared to leave a complete message when the party is not in. Ask for the floor plans and fact sheets to be sent to you. Granted, you will not always be successful in getting this information as some spaces have never been built and do not have space plans or what are also referred to as as-built drawings. Not getting as much information on these spaces ahead of time will waste your time and your money by keeping you away from what you do best to be profitable.

You will want to see the properties that most closely meet your needs. But first, it is important to be prepared to ask the right questions before going out on a visit. I suggest that you make a list from your planning goals used to define your requirements and put them in order of importance. A simple ranking system will do. Put a three next to anything you cannot live without, a two next to anything that is very important but you might be able to work around, such a re-configuring the space in some way and finally, a one next to anything that is desirable but not necessary. By doing it this way you can use a higher point system to decide which properties to visit first, which are on your second tier list and which ones to eliminate. You will also want to collect the economic information and put it into a format that makes the best sense for you to understand and to later rely on. This table is a sample of a system that we employ for our clients:

Property Information for:						XYZ Corporation				
Prioritized Items:				Key:	FS:	Full Service; All utilities and cleaning is provided in the rate				
SubMarket:	North Fulton/Alpharetta/Roswell				MG:	Modified Gross; Tenant usually pays for electric and cleaning				
Size:	4500 - 6000 Square Feet				NNN:	Triple Net; Tenant Pays for all utilities, CAM charges and cleaning				
Building Class:	Class "B+/A-" Space				SF:	Square Feet				
Space Layout:	8 Offices/Conference/Break/Open Area for 20 Cubes									
Lease Term:	3-5 year Lease									
Building Address		Rentable Office SF	Quoted $/SF	Lease Type	Rent per Month	Effective Rent/Mo	Build Out Allowance	Total Allowance	New Space	Additional Comments
123	Alparetta Hwy	4,755	$19.00	FS	$7,528	$7,528.75	$10.00	$47,550.00	No	Available 20 Months
123	Crabapple	4,785	$21.00	FS	$8,373	$8,373.75	$10.00	$47,850.00	Yes	Listed for 35 Months
234	Freedom Parkway	5,000	$24.00	FS	$10,000	$10,000.00	$10.00	$50,000.00	No	Available 4 Months
567	Highway 9	5,236	$25.00	FS	$10,908	$10,908.33	$10.00	$52,360.00	No	Available 18 Months
678	Holcomb Bridge	4,896	$29.00	FS	$11,832	$11,832.00	$10.00	$48,960.00	No	Available 7 Months
Averages		5,371	$23.02		$10,317	$10,317.68	$13.68	$73,481.30		

As you can see, the information contained above is vital to have so that you can negotiate from a position of strength. But, before you can begin to make calls on properties, you will need to understand a few basics about lease rental rates and how space is actually measured.

CHAPTER 11

Understanding Rental Rates

B ecause there are a number of factors that compromise rents and several customary ways to quote rents, it can be difficult to understand what people mean when they are discussing leasing rates. Normally, the rate quoted reflects the amount of rent you pay per square foot. Generally square foot prices are quoted on an annual basis. For example, a $36.00 per square foot annual rate is equal to a $3.00 per square foot monthly rate. While this is simple math, it can come as a bit of a shock sometimes when you hear a rate quoted for one space as $3.00 per foot and another as $36.00.

The rate quoting style tends to vary: urban office leasing is generally quoted as an annual rate. Also important to note is that real estate brokers commonly refer to annual square foot rates while the tenants often look at the rates as monthly. This difference may occur because each uses the rate differently. Tenants commonly look at their expenses from a monthly expense perspective, while agents deal in leasing agreements in annual terms. Aside from different usage of square footage there are key attributes associated with each square foot rate.

These attributes are most commonly referred to as: <u>Full Service Gross</u>, <u>Modified Gross</u> (or Single Net), and <u>Triple Net</u> (or Absolute Net); all of these except the Full Service Gross rent may have Common Area Maintenance (CAM) charges added on. On the property fact sheet above you may see these written as; FSG, MG, N, NNN, CAM. These attributes determine who pays the utilities, janitorial and other building services (elevators, common hall lights, etc.) and are key factors in determining the true asking rate.

- <u>Full Service Gross rental rate</u> is generally associated with urban or multi-tenant office buildings indicating that the asking rate includes all the building services, utilities and janitorial, property taxes, insurance, and common area maintenance.

- <u>Net rental rate</u> generally indicates what the asking rate does not cover. For example net of utilities and janitorial means that the tenant is, at a minimum responsible for their own utilities, janitorial, plus the base rent. There is nothing about leasing that causes more confusion than the term Net because it is so often misused, even by otherwise competent brokers. So let me make this really easy for you and save you some real grief later. When you hear the word Net, think of the word "not", or in other words, something is not included in the rent. You then need to ask this question: "Please tell me all the things I will be paying for that are not included in the rent." This will be essential in comparing the final cost of leasing one property over another.

- <u>Triple Net rental rate</u> (sometimes called absolute net) is also commonly used in retail leasing or with freestanding, single tenant property. In this case the tenant will pay for all the services, the taxes and insurance plus any maintenance to the roof, foundations, sidewalls, and all building systems.

- <u>Common Area Maintenance</u> charges are sometimes added to the quoted rate and most often found in industrial parks and smaller strip retail centers. They refer to the cost of maintaining the parking lot, sidewalks, landscaping, signs or any other assets used in common by the tenants.

Before you begin any site inspections, it is important to understand some basic concepts about commercial space. The first is that commercial space often needs to be modified to meet the needs of the tenant and rarely do the existing conditions of space precisely meet the needs of the incoming tenant. Landlords anticipate this and are prepared to negotiate improvements for the tenant. How much can you successfully negotiate is a question of market conditions. Higher vacancy rates in a given market translate into more landlord contribution and conversely, very tight markets can put the responsibility to customize the space on the incoming tenant. Later we will discuss the space planning aspects of your transactions, but first we need to gain greater knowledge of how commercial space is measured before we go out and start visiting available space.

CHAPTER 12

How Space Is Measured

While all properties use the square foot as the basis of measurement, which parts of the property are included in the final calculations vary by building type. Gross square footage is most typically used with warehouses, industrial buildings and other stand- alone buildings such as freestanding retail sites. Typically, the calculation will include the thickness of the sidewalls when measuring the total footprint of the site. This measurement will include 50% of the thickness of any demising walls. The actual square footage that an office user may occupy is typically less than the amount upon which the rent is based. The square footage that you use exclusively is termed "usable square feet". This is because office tenants pay their proportionate share for their use of building common areas. Common areas include lobbies, hallways, rest rooms, and service areas. The differential is expressed as a percentage known as a load factor. When comparing properties, it's a good idea to ask, "What is the load factor?" The higher the load factor the more of your space will be in the common areas and less inside the suite for your exclusive use. Occasionally, one may find a building that bases the rent upon the usable square footage. Since load factors can run 12 to 22 percent, this may represent real savings.

How does the load factor affect the economics of a lease transaction? The higher the load factor, the more space you need to rent in order to occupy an equal amount of usable space. When using a broker, ask for a lease analysis of both the rentable and the usable square footage.

There are standards by which commercial space is measured. In many areas, commercial property owners adhere to the Building Owners' and Manager's Association (BOMA) standard. BOMA standards offer guidelines as to where and how to measure certain areas of property. For example, to determine the measurement point on an exterior wall, the architect must determine the dominant portion of the wall. It could be the glass line or the wall surface depending upon the portion of the wall that comprises more than 50% of the wall's surface.

In multi-tenant buildings or on multi-tenant floors, hallways, maintenance areas, and rest rooms are apportioned to the tenants and are either included in the rentable area calculations or included in the common area maintenance charges. Vertical penetrations such as stairwells, elevators and utility shafts are not included. These are just a few examples of the BOMA standards. Always ask how the space has been measured and about the load factor to ensure you get the benefit of your bargain.

CHAPTER 13

Space Configuration Effects Efficiency

Comparing window and column spacing as it pertains to your needs can affect the efficiency of various office and R&D buildings. While there are many buildings that are effectively column free, often column spacing needs to be considered.

An office plan that calls for a high percentage of interior partition walls can integrate columns well into the plan, often affording striking design elements. While open plan users may find that too many columns can increase the cost of furniture systems and increase their square footage requirements. Window spacing has a minimal effect on open plan office users. However, private office intensive users need to look closely at how window spacing affects office sizes, particularly where a mixture of office sizes is desired. The dividers between windows are referred to as mullions. The difference between 4 foot 6 inch mullion spacing and a 5 foot mullion can be dramatic. By example, a three windowed office would measure 13 feet 5 inches and 15 feet, respectively, resulting in an 11% difference in office size without a substantial benefit in usability.

STAGE III

4-3 MONTHS AWAY: Property Review

Well, you've eliminated some of the spaces on your list and you should have at least 10 spaces that fit into your planning goals. You've done the market research and have a good understanding of the market you wish to locate your business. You know which projects are available and how much space is vacant. You know the rates and the improvement allowances. You've taken a cursory look at space plans and through your rating system have decided that there are about 10 spaces that actually warrant your time for consideration. Now is the time when you should get into your car and look at the individual spaces.

CHAPTER 14

Touring Properties

Depending on how good a job you or your broker have done in the pre-qualifying process, this task can be as fun or as arduous as you all make it. Your objective during these tours will be to evaluate floor locations, views, physical characteristics, amenities, as well as the general character and quality of the building or site. Check the overall condition of the improvements that already exist for level of workmanship. Remember, you will occupy this space for the next 5 – 10 years and you might as well establish the baseline on your terms up front. Look at the conditions of the grounds and parking lot. This may be a reflection as to what type of project as well as what type of owner you will, or will not be dealing with. Use the Tour Site Checklist (see appendix) to facilitate a thorough comparison of the buildings, this checklist can help you to evaluate non-economic aspects of the sites you visit. It also assists you in recalling the details of the properties and in narrowing down the list. There are some key elements to consider when visiting potential spaces.

1. **Visit Space on Your Schedule.** It is important to note at this point that the world revolves around you. That's right, the world revolves around you. You are the customer; you are the one taking the risk; you are the person that is taking time away from his primary business to look at the landlord's office space. You should make sure that this process fits around your schedule. Try to set up your inspection tours in groups of three to four buildings at a time, about 30-60 minutes per property plus travel time will be sufficient. By limiting each tour to 3 or 4 properties you can more readily compare the features and benefits each while maintaining clarity and separation between the properties in your mind. A tour with more than 4 properties at one time can become unproductive. Bringing a camera helps too, in remembering the space beyond a small floor plan, as does taking notes.

2. **Examine the Condition and Maintenance of the Exterior of the Project.** Unkempt landscaping, trash sitting around dumpsters, poorly maintained parking lots, crumbling building exteriors, visibly filthy windows are but a few of the concerns that you should look for when approaching and walking into a project. Take a look at the corridors and the restrooms of every project you visit. Are lights out in the corridors or in the space itself? The overall condition of the project will go a long way to describing how the space will be kept as well as the landlord's overall effort in maintaining the building you are considering spending the next 5-10 years.

3. **Examine the Level of Finishes.** Along the same lines of looking at the exterior of the project for the level of maintenance that you should expect at each project, you should also do the same with the finishes within the building.

Shabby workmanship shows easily and is an indication of a landlord that is willing to cut corners at the expense of your happiness. Outdated carpeting or tile in the premises, hallways, or restrooms is a strong sign that the landlord is, well, cheap, or at least poorly funded. Walls that don't align or ceiling tiles that are tan instead of white due to age also support the idea that you may want to look elsewhere for your office space.

4. **Is the Space Comfortable?** Nothing upsets most office staff more than an uncomfortable office. Not to mention the fact that an uncomfortable staff is an unproductive staff. You need to have an understanding of the temperature in the office during various times of the workday. You need to know who is in control of the temperature as well as what happens to the air conditioner after normal business hours. If temperature-wise, you are uncomfortable in an office space you are viewing, you may want to pass on the space.

5. **Is the Building Secure?** Unfortunately, making sure that security exists after business hours end is a way of life today. Whether the landlord provides a security guard or a system, they need to provide some sort of program to ensure your security. You need to have an understanding of which security services should be provided by you and which by the Landlord.

6. **Does the Building Meet your Planning and Goals?** After completing the Tour Site Checklist, the answer to this question should be clearer than when you started the tour. It is important not to skip over items in this checklist in the interest of brevity. Something that may be considered trivial

and not worth writing down today may be an important factor later and if not written down will force you to have to revisit the space at the expense of your time. The checklist has been developed and used with the reality that anyone can use this worksheet. So take every advantage of using it to its fullest extent.

Now that you've completed the silent review, there is some pertinent information that you will need to ask the Landlord during this process.

CHAPTER 15

Questions You Might Be Asked

When you are touring potential locations to lease, you are likely to be asked some qualifying questions. You might want to think about what information you are prepared to give up and what you will want to hold back. In a negotiation, information is king and giving up too much too quickly can compromise your bargaining power, especially if time is short. Some typical reasonable questions are listed below:

- When does your lease expire?
- What is your budget?
- What else have you seen?
- Are you working with any brokers?
- Why do you have to move?
- Do you have any other options?
- Where does the company leadership or employee base live?
- Who are the other decision-makers?
- What is your business history?
- What is your financial condition?
- What are you growth plans?
- What doesn't work about the space you have now?

STAGE IV

3-2 MONTHS AWAY: Proposal/Negotiation Stage

After reviewing several properties and uncovering 3-4 that you believe will fit your goals, now is the time to start making your proposal(s), as the case may be. Because you are making non-binding proposals, you should feel comfortable to make more than one proposal at a time. In many areas of the country it is an accepted practice to do so. You must be careful that the property owner does not incur significant expenses on your behalf or he may have recourse against you for those expenses if you fail to consummate a lease. I'd advise you not to go much beyond the first round of proposal responses or into multiple space planning sessions without informing the property owners that you are negotiating for more than one space. Creating competition in a softer market can work well to your advantage, so letting the other side know that you have other options can garner some nice concessions. Just be careful and let the other party know that you are continuing to consider other locations.

Most often, proposals to lease commercial property take the form of a letter of intent. A letter of intent outlines the basic terms under which the parties would enter into a lease contract. Moreover, the Letter of Intent allows you to dictate the terms you are willing to accept to the Landlord as opposed to waiting for the Landlord to give you the same information you already know…wasting your valuable time. I don't ask for what I know the landlord will accept. I always demand more than my client wants and if necessary we settle for more than they need.

There are basically two approaches that brokers use in preparing letters of intent. The approach I favor is to make the proposal simple. That means I'll try to gain agreement on the big issues first and set aside smaller issues to work out later in the lease negotiations. I prefer this strategy in negotiations because it relieves much of the inherent tension in the negotiations and makes agreement on the side issues easier to obtain. Some brokers prefer to issue a very lengthy letter of intent, covering every conceivable issue up front. I feel that this can dampen the spirit of the negotiations and often hit a hot button on a minor point. I've seen too many landlords get vexed about minor side issues, and subsequently fail to see the merits of the proposal. After all the terms are settled, the credit-worthiness evaluated, and conditions satisfied, a lease draft is prepared.

CHAPTER 16

The Letter of Intent Proposal

As previously discussed, there are several methods of relaying your goals and needs to the Landlord.

I prefer that you take the initiative in this process by controlling the initial offer. An example of a typical offer is shown below:

August 29, 2003

Ms. Mary Smith
Smith Management Corp.
3200 Pointe Tower Place, Suite 3502
Your Town, USA 87654

Re: Offer from XYZ Corporation to Lease Office Space at: Tower Pointe Office Park, 456 Tower Pointe Road, Suite 2400, Your Town, USA 98765

Dear Mary,

On behalf of my client, XYZ Corporation, I am enclosing a proposal to lease the above referenced professional office building.

Please review the attached proposal as my client is actively searching for space. If, after a review of the attached, there are any questions regarding these terms, or any other issues, please call me.

Sincerely,
The Miller Group, LLC

Robert A. Miller, CCIM, RPA
President

XYZ Corporation Lease PROPOSAL

Business Terms

PREMISES: Tower Pointe Office Center
456 Tower Pointe Road,   Suite 2400
Your Town, USA 98765

SPACE   ± 5455 Rentable Square Feet, to be confirmed by
Landlord's architect using BOMA standards

LESSEE: XYZ Corporation, Inc., A Delaware Corporation

LESSOR: Vacancy Partners, LLC

COMMENCEMENT DATE: Lease to begin on or before:
April 1, 2003.

LEASE TERM: 72 Months

LEASE RATE: $19.75/R.S.F.

LEASE TYPE: Full Service Gross

LEASE STRUCTURE:

Lease Term	Annual Base Rental	Monthly Base Rental
April 1, 2003 - March 31, 2004	$107,736.25	$8,978.02
April 1, 2004 - March 31, 2005	$110,968.34	$9,247.36
April 1, 2005 - March 31, 2006	$114,297.39	$9,524.78
April 1, 2006 - March 31, 2007	$117,726.31	$9,810.53
April 1, 2007 - March 31, 2008	$121,258.10	$10,104.84

ANNUAL ESCALATIONS: 3%

SECURITY DEPOSIT: $10,000.00

BASE YEAR: 2003

LESSEE IMPROVEMENT

ALLOWANCE: Owner shall provide tenant improvements in accordance with a mutually acceptable space plan, which plan shall be provided at Owner's sole expense. It is contemplated that the Tenant's improvements shall include the following items of improvement:

1. The premises shall be re-carpeted.

2. The premises shall be repainted per Lessee's requirements with a maximum of three (3) colors used.

3. Lessor shall provide Crown Molding in all Managerial offices.

LESSOR CONCESSIONS:

1. Lessor shall provide Lessee a Movement Allowance of up to $12000.00.

2. Lessor shall provide Lessee Free Rent for a period of no less than twelve (12) months at the commencement of this Lease.

3. Lessor shall provide Lessee a first right of refusal for any adjacent contiguous space for the purpose of expansion. Lessee shall have ninety (90) days to respond in writing to the Lessor of its intentions.

RENEWAL OPTIONS: Provided the Lessee has not been in

continuing default during the term of the Lease, Lessor shall provide Lessee two (2) options to renew this Lease for at least 60 months. The rate will be the lesser of current market rent(s) or 103% of the existing term rental.

LESSOR SERVICES:

1. HVAC: The minimum hours of HVAC operation are from 7:00 am to 7:00 pm Monday through Friday and from 9:00 am to 4:00 pm on Saturdays.

2. Electrical: Lessor provides electrical service as part of the Lease rate.

3. Janitorial: Lessor provides a bonded janitorial service 5 nights per week.

4. Equipment: N/A

PARKING: Lessor to provide a 4/1000 parking ratio.

ACCESS: Lessee shall have 24 hours/day, 7 days/week, 52-weeks year access to the Premises, the building and the parking facilities.

SECURITY: The premises provides abundant outside lighting including street lighting, building wall packs and parking lot lights.

SIGNAGE: Lessor to provide, at no charge to Lessee, signage in accordance with corporate park standards. Any additional signage must have written permission from the Lessor.

DISCLOSURE: In accordance with the Georgia Real estateDisclosure Law, the Lessee is represented by The Miller Group, LLC and shall be compensated equal to two (2) months rental and four percent (4%) of the total rental value of this Lease. Smith Management represents the Lessor in this transaction. The Lessor shall compensate the broker(s) per separate agreement.

MISCELLANEOUS: This proposal is subject to the availability of the property, the users compliance with municipal ordinances, financials of tenant, and a mutually agreed upon building layout.

This proposal is subject to review after 30 days.

This proposal represents some of our understandings about a possible future Sublease and is not intended to create a legally binding obligation on either party. Such an obligation will be created only when both parties execute a formal Sublease, covering all of the rights and obligations of the parties, which is then delivered by and between Lessee and Lessor.

Now lets breakdown what is shown above and why it is important to include this information:

XYZ Corporation Lease PROPOSAL

We can see that this opening defines the parties and identifies the property.

PREMISES: Tower Pointe Office Center
456 Tower Pointe Road,   Suite 2400
Your Town, USA 98765

The key here is to make sure that as much of the project as possible is identified

SPACE: ± 5455 Rentable Square Feet, to be confirmed by Landlord's architect using BOMA standards

We would use this type of description when the Premises we desire are not yet demised or we desire a portion of a larger suite that can be made smaller.

LESSEE: XYZ Corporation, Inc., A Delaware Corporation

Always use the legal name of your business because the owner may respond differently if you are signing personally or as a corporation, LLP or LLC.

LESSOR: Vacancy Partners, LLC

Always use the legal name of the Landlord's entity so you know what entity to sue later. I'm not kidding here. It also establishes what party is responsible for getting this deal completed as well as the party responsible for providing its agreed upon services to you.

COMMENCEMENT DATE: Lease to begin on or before: April 1, 2003

If there is a date by which you must absolutely occupy the premises, then add, "But in no case later than (date)". If the premises must be remodeled then we would insert the phrase "Or upon substantial completion of the tenant improvements"

LEASE TERM: 72 Months

Simply dictates what the initial term of the lease your organization will accept.

LEASE TYPE: Full Service Gross

This states to the Landlord what type of lease you will engage in as well as further delineating what type of services you expect the Landlord should perform. We've already covered in detail (Chapter 9) what type of services this Lease type should entail.

LEASE STRUCTURE:

Lease Term	Annual Base Rental	Monthly Base Rental
April 1, 2003 - March 31, 2004	$107,736.25	$8,978.02
April 1, 2004 - March 31, 2005	$110,968.34	$9,247.36
April 1, 2005 - March 31, 2006	$114,297.39	$9,524.78
April 1, 2006 - March 31, 2007	$117,726.31	$9,810.53
April 1, 2007 - March 31, 2008	$121,258.10	$10,104.84

It is always smart to identify and produce the rental schedule so that you are in control of this portion of the process as well as have a better understanding of what the lease rate translates to on a monthly and annual basis.

Owners expect that the first months' rent will be paid upon lease execution even if there are several months before the commencement date.

Negotiation Tip: If you are leasing more space than you need intentionally you may be able to structure the rent so that it starts off lower and graduates. OR, you might ask that the first year's rent be calculated only on the portion of the space that you will be using initially.

ANNUAL ESCALATIONS: 3%

This is the basis is for annual rent payment increases and is reflected in the lease structure previously shown. Many companies like using Government's Consumer Price Index as a basis for rate increases but it is a difficult measure to rely on for budgeting purposes. If you are comfortable with using the CPI as a basis for rate increases and you are confident it will be less than a fixed amount during the term of your lease, by all means, use CPI as your escalator.

SECURITY DEPOSIT: $10,000.00

Landlords will in most cases require a security deposit to help offset the potential additional expenses incurred, upon the end of the lease, for excess wear and damage to the Premises. This is not to be used as the last months' rent although often, this amount will coincide with that figure. Also, your credit strength may dictate this amount. That is why it is important to identify what you will be willing to offer (if anything at all) for a deposit.

BASE YEAR: 2003

Tenants are usually required to pay for any increases in the cost of operating the building after the first year of the lease. This is more fully explained later in the book. The first year of the lease is called the base year, because it is the year to which all future operating expense budgets are compared. Base years are most often calendar years especially in multi-tenant property.

LESSEE IMPROVEMENT
ALLOWANCE: Owner shall provide tenant improvements

in accordance with a mutually acceptable space plan, which plan shall be provided at Owner's sole expense. It is contemplated that the Tenant's improvements shall include the following items of improvement:

1. The premises shall be re-carpeted.

2. The premises shall be repainted per Lessee's requirements with a maximum of three (3) colors used.

3. Lessor shall provide Crown Molding in all Managerial offices.

Here you would list the modifications you want. This example is a simple improvement to an existing space that has specific issues for already identified offices and the rest of the Premises. For spaces that are new, you will need to enlist the aid of a space planner and you may want to have the owner provide the preliminary space planning services. If you are providing your own space planner, it is not unreasonable to negotiate for payment of your architect by the owner. Typically, this would occur when space-planning services are already being offered by the owner to attract tenants. It's worth a try.

Some buildings offer a Tenant Improvement Allowance. This is stated as a number of dollars per square foot. These can range from enough to provide paint and carpet to a full build-out.

Since office buildings quote the rent on rentable basis, it makes sense that the Tenant Improvement Allowance is also quoted that way. But often it is not, particularly in new construction, because the common areas have to be developed by the owner and a portion of the allowance is used for that. Ask how the Tenant Improvement Allowance is quoted to be sure of what you are getting. If the allowance or other tenant improvement package offered is less than you need to construct your premises then negotiate for more. If the Landlord is unwilling to add more funds to meet your needs, have the market knowledge to justify why they should submit to your requirements. If that doesn't work, consider paying for the overage yourself and get the Landlord to reduce his rental rates. The tax benefits of depreciating the cost over the term of your lease to your organization combined with the offset of lower rental rates may be worth considering. The final option is to ask that the excess improvements be amortized over the term of the lease. This is effectively a loan to you and will increase your monthly rent and will normally bear interest at the owner's cost of funds or slightly more.

Note that if the owner is doing the work of improvement based upon an allowance, they will be taking some back for supervision of that task on your behalf, this can range from 5% to 15% and is negotiable. Ask if there will be a supervision charge when you are quoted an allowance and negotiate this amount down. Architectural and engineering costs will be also taken from the allowance and can run from $1.50 to $2.50 per square foot.

Be aware that if you are offered a reimbursement for tenant improvements provided by you, it could cause a taxable event. Consult a tax advisor before agreeing to any cash allowance that comes as a reimbursement. An example of how to write this may be:

LESSEE IMPROVEMENT ALLOWANCE: Owner shall provide a tenant improvement allowance of $25.00 per rentable square foot and shall construct the Premises in accordance with a mutually acceptable space plan, which plan shall be provided at Owner's sole expense. It is contemplated that the Tenant's improvements shall include the following items of improvement:

(Here you would list the improvements you want)

Supervision fees charged by Owner shall be limited to X% of the cost of improvement work.

TIP: If you've been provided with a floor plan of existing conditions, mark it up and include it with you proposal.

A final note on tenant improvements: Sometimes you will hear the term "Tenant Work Letter", most often this will be in conjunction with new developments. This refers to a list of building standard component parts that are used to develop the premises for the prospective tenant. Typically, this is allocated as a certain number of each item for each 100 to 150 square feet of space leased. By example: a certain number of lineal feet of wall per 100 square feet, one electrical outlet per 150 square feet, one phone outlet, one interior door, so many sprinkler heads and so on. While this can be confusing, the solution is quite simple. Proceed to space planning, which will be discussed in-depth later in the book, and have the architect tell you if the "work letter" is sufficient to create the suite you desire/ If not, you're back to the negotiating table for what you want. The next thing that we need to cover is some of the concessions available to you.

Concessions are anything beyond what the standard offers as Landlord standards. Think of these items like buying a base model car at a fixed price but adding a sunroof, CD player, free maintenance, leather seats and upgraded wheels all for the same base model rate. The same idea applies to office leasing when a Landlord has too much available office space. A few concessions that we generally employ are shown below.

LESSOR CONCESSIONS:

1. Lessor shall provide Lessee a Movement Allowance of up to $12000.00.

Negotiation tip: Depending upon the Landlord's vacancy and economic situation, they may be more apt to provide this concession to you.

2. Lessor shall provide Lessee Free Rent for a period of no less than twelve (12) months at the commencement of this Lease.

Negotiation tip: The owner might be more willing to grant rent abatement if you propose ½ rent for a longer time rather than free rent for a shorter period. Free rent can also be spread out over the term, which is often more palatable to owners.

3. Lessor shall provide Lessee a first right of refusal for any adjacent contiguous space for the purpose of expansion. Lessee shall have ninety (90) days to respond in writing to the Lessor of its intentions.

Most tenants are concerned about expansion rights so they can avoid moving if they outgrow the space. Owners are reluctant to grant any options since options never serve the owner's interests. I suggest you ask for more than what you want but expect that the owner's response will attempt to water down your right as much as possible.

Here's a straightforward way of obtaining the right to renew the lease without having to guess at the future rental rate.

RENEWAL OPTIONS: Provided the Lessee has not been in continuing default during the term of the Lease, Lessor shall provide Lessee two (2) options to renew this Lease for at least 60 months. The rate will be the lesser of 95% of the verifiable current market rent(s) or 103% of the existing term rental.

As you can see, you can choose to negotiate for a fixed rate increase in the renewal or a CPI index adjustment, or a fair market value adjustment. The clause would be modified accordingly.

LESSOR SERVICES:

1. HVAC: The minimum hours of HVAC operation are from 7:00 am to 7:00 pm Monday through Friday and from 9:00 am to 4:00 pm on Saturdays.

2. Electrical: Lessor provides electrical service as part of the Lease rate.

3. Janitorial: Lessor provides a bonded janitorial service 5 nights per week.

4. Equipment: N/A

It is imperative that you identify what services the Landlord shall provide versus what you think he may provide. There is no need to be ambiguous here. Specify what you need to be done within the lease type that you are working with.

PARKING: Lessor to provide free parking at a 4/1000 parking ratio.

This is an area that must be identified and agreed upon early. For regular surface parking that has no cost to the Tenant, the key item is to identify what is the minimum number that you may require for your particular space. This number can rise or fall based on need. If, for example, you are a call center or a residential real estate agency you will require a greater number of parking space per 1000 square feet. Conversely, a law firm may require less parking.

The key element issue is to identify who pays for parking. In suburban markets, parking will often be free because of the type of buildings and parking that are in a suburban market. In urban or downtown markets, the Landlord, especially in major cities, will have a cost for each space that is required. This rate is often negotiable but you must know what that figure translates to and what economic impact that will have on your business and your employees.

ACCESS: Lessee shall have 24 hours/day, 7 days/week, 52-weeks/year access to the Premises, the building and the parking facilities.

You need to ensure that you have access to the premises you are renting 24 hours a day regardless of holidays or weekends. Why? You are paying for the premises everyday you occupy the space.

SECURITY: The premises provides abundant outside lighting including street lighting, building wall packs and parking lot lights.

This is of paramount importance to you and your associates. Identifying what shall be required to ensure the safety of your staff, your clients and yourself are non-negotiable issues. Dictating to the landlord what the minimum requirements shall be will ensure that you will get what you want.

SIGNAGE: Lessor to provide, at no charge to Lessee, signage in accordance with corporate park standards. Any additional signage must have written permission from the Lessor.

More often than not, the Landlord will expect to pay for a minimum number of signs. Whether they are on an entry monument or at the entrance to the premises, make sure that the Landlord covers the cost of this.

If, based on the size and term you are proposing, you believe that you should have the opportunity to place your company's name and logo on the building, this would be a good place to locate that requirement.

DISCLOSURE: In accordance with the Georgia Real estate Disclosure Law, the Lessee is represented by The Miller Group, LLC and shall be compensated equal to two (2) months rental and four percent (4%) of the total rental value of this Lease. Smith Management represents the Lessor in this transaction. The Lessor shall compensate the broker(s) per separate agreement.

In the event a broker is involved, as well as depending upon each state's real estate commission requirements, it is important to disclose up front who is to compensate whom as well as who represents whom if applicable. Always demand that the Landlord pay any commissions due to any real estate broker involved in your transaction.

MISCELLANEOUS: This proposal is subject to the availability of the property, the users compliance with municipal ordinances, financials of tenant, and a mutually agreed upon building layout.

This proposal is subject to review after 30 days.

This proposal represents some of our understandings about a possible future Sublease and is not intended to create a legally binding obligation for either party. Such an obligation will be created only when both parties execute a formal Sublease, covering all of the rights and obligations of the parties, which is then delivered by and between Lessee and Lessor.

For the proposal to be constructed as non-binding, it is essential that it be clearly stated that there are additional matters that bear further negotiation. It is not enough to just say this is non-binding. This proposal will get you well into the lease negotiations. Once the proposal stage is complete, you will be provided with a draft lease for you and your legal counsel to review and fine tune into a contract that accurately defines your agreement. Please do not construe the information provided here as legal advice or as a substitute for legal advice. This is intended to be a primer in the negotiation phase.

CHAPTER 17

Lease Negotiations to Lease Execution

ANALYSIS OF RESPONSE TO PROPOSALS

After the owner has responded to your initial proposal, it is time to analyze all the major points of the response. If you have made more than one proposal there are certain elements that need to be compared. These items might include:

- Rent change calculated on the basis of rentable square feet and the rental rate calculated on the basis of useable square feet. This is arrived at by subtracting the load factor from the rentable square footage.

- Compare the effective rent, which is nothing more than averaging all the years of the rent and factoring in any free rent periods. This is important because your responses may use different rent structures. By reducing this to the average rent per year, per foot, you can easily see which proposal has the better economics.

- Different properties have differing operating expense histories and it is a good idea to ask for a 3-year history of the operating expenses. Well-run buildings have very stable operating expense histories and unless there's been a spike in energy costs, janitorial contract re-negotiations, or an insurance crisis, the expenses should be fairly even.

Next you will want to compare:

- Tenant improvements offered by the owner
- The cost of any improvements you are required to provide
- Length of term, options to extend or renew
- Timing to delivery
- Overall suitability

RESPONSES BACK FROM OUR PROPOSALS

The negotiation of the lease document is one of the most crucial steps in the relocation process. Because there are almost as many lease contracts as there are buildings to lease, it is impractical and inadvisable to sign a lease contract without a review by qualified legal counsel. Some leases are preprinted forms, which may be suitable for many transactions, most are customized contracts developed by the legal counsel for the landlord. Preprinted form leases can run from two legal size pages to sixteen pages, plus addenda and exhibits. Custom leases, especially for office buildings can easily run 50 to 80 pages. All leases define the business terms, which is the smallest portion of the lease. The balance of the lease seeks to contemplate possible future events and prepares for these events.

You will need to work closely with your broker and/or legal counsel (if applicable) in negotiating the final terms of the lease, including the language of the lease, the economics of the lease, all references to the interior construction and other contractual elements. The competent broker that you have contracted with should know all of the current issues regarding the lease as well as how to overcome many of the objections you and the Landlord may have. Make sure that all the terms of the proposals are incorporated in to the lease and reviewed every step of the way. Next we will develop a basic understanding of how to deal with some of the more common clauses in the contract.

CHAPTER 18

Common Lease Clauses

THE PARTIES TO THE LEASE

Your lease will start off with the basic business points, either in an outline form or using a fill-in-the-blanks system as with form leases. We do need to know some of the nuances of these. The lease will describe the legal entities involved in the transaction, but, you need to make sure that this is correctly done, as mistakes here can be costly. If your business is a corporation or limited liability company, you certainly want to maintain the protection that these business structures afford.

PREMISES

Next will be a description of the premises. Some forms define both the rentable and usable square footage; others just give the suite number and refer to an exhibit, which is an architectural drawing of the space. Always ask how recently the space was measured and by whom. When an architect is involved, it should be easy to obtain accurate area calculations.

TERM AND COMMENCEMENT

The term may be the next item and includes the commencement date, expiration date and contemplates a possible delay in possession. If the space you are leasing is vacant and in move-in condition, you will most likely not have any issues with a delay in possession of the premises. If the space is subject to construction work, you may need to anticipate delays, or even establish a "drop-dead-date".

When does a commercial lease actually start? There are a number of factors that can delay possession of the lease premises. Depending on the cause of the delay, the lease term and rent obligations may or may not commence on the date set forth in the lease. Let's look first at a situation where a newly leased premise is already occupied and the existing tenant delays his departure. Under the typical lease, the owner would have no liability to the new tenant for such a delay. The new tenant's only recourse may be to wait it out, until a "drop dead date" is reached or the premise is delivered. The "drop dead date" is the date by which, if the premises are not delivered, a tenant has the right to cancel a lease negotiable item, but 60 to 180 days is typical. Frequently, a delay in possession does not extend the term of the lease, leaving the tenant with a shorter term than anticipated. Be sure that any delay in possession automatically extends the expiration of the lease term to get the full benefit of your bargain.

Let's now take a look at a leasing situation where the owner has assumed the responsibility of providing tenant improvements. Here, there are many potential delays possible. Delays caused by circumstances outside the owner's control such as strikes, weather, governmental procedures, fires or other accidents extend the commencement date and the "drop dead date" without liability to the owner. In all the preceding examples no rent would be payable unless the premises is actually delivered.

However, delays caused by the tenant in approving plans, making payments for work performed on the tenant's account, or resulting from change orders by tenant, are not the responsibilities of the owner. This type of delay in possession may start the rent and other tenant obligations prior to occupancy.

You are also likely to encounter the term "Substantially Complete" with respect to the owner's delivery of the premises. This is intended to mean ready to occupy, with only a punch-list of items to be completed or corrected.

USE

The use clause will appear with the basic business points and is important, because if too tightly written, it can affect what you are permitted to do in the premises later if your businesses model changes and your rights to sublease or assign the lease at a later time. Think about the ramifications of this clause with respect to your business.

Many leases seek to distance the owner from any liability about the suitability of your intended use of the premises. In fact it is your responsibility to have checked out the zoning and permitting process before you sign a lease and begin to operate your business in the location. Before signing any lease you must go to the governing authority and ensure that you can get the necessary license.

RENT CLAUSES

Depending on the type of lease you are working with, the rent will very likely cover a number of clauses. First, the base rent will be stated along with any negotiated increases or CPI increases. Subsequent clauses will deal with who pays which expenses. For example, if the tenant pays the expense directly or reimburses the owner for actual expenses, there will be a clause to cover that aspect of the lease. Where the owner pays a particular expense as part of the base rent, he will seek to protect those costs from increasing.

OPERATING EXPENSE INCREASES

We've discussed the various kinds of rent structures common to leasing, but wait there's still more. It often comes as a surprise to tenants to find out that the rent they have negotiated is subject to various kinds of increases. The most common is the requirement to pay for increases in the owner's share of the costs of operating the building, and sometimes tenants object to this. Since this can rarely be negotiated away, let's take some time to understand this. The basic principle here is, when expenses are included in the rent they are subject to increases if the cost of providing those services increases over the term of the lease. Many of these services are a direct benefit to the tenant such as utilities, janitorial, maintenance and elevator service contracts. Some, like real estate taxes and owner's policy of insurance are not, but the payments for any increase in these expenses are borne by the tenant in most leases. Let's look at why.

Commercial property income is under constant attack from the erosive effects of time, government regulation and increased operating costs. After the taxes, insurance and operating expenses have been paid from recent receipts; the money remaining is the net income, commonly referred to as the Net Operating Income or the N.O.I. The N.O.I is used for several important calculations, including a computation known as the Capitalization Rate, or Cap Rate. The Cap Rate is used to estimate the property value and determine the refinance-ability or value of the property. Prudent property owners seek to block the erosion of the Net Operating Income to prevent a decline in property value. Likewise, increasing the Net Operating Income increases the property value.

There are many erosive forces at work that can silently reduce a commercial property value. Property taxes increase annually, insurance costs constantly creep up, utilities and other operating expenses must be monitored and re-negotiated. The lease contract rent, which is a promise to pay, is paid in future dollars. Inflation causes the future value of money to have less purchasing power. That is why the commercial lease contract contains protective clauses against income erosion. These are known as escalation clauses.

One such clause is the Operating Expense Increase clause, which can go by other names, such as Additional Rent. It allows the property owner to pass through increases of operating expenses to the commercial tenant. Normally, the pass through begins in the second year of the lease term. The first year of the lease term is referred to as the Base Year or Comparison Year. Increased expenses are compared to the Base Year and the difference is apportioned to all the tenants and "passed through" as an operating expense increase. There are numerous variations to how this lease clause is constructed, outlining the specifics of how and when these sums are to be paid. Frequently, increases in operating expenses are estimated in advance, based upon a budget, and are collected monthly as additional rent. To protect against tax and insurance increases most leases use a base year similar to the operating expense base year. However, a tax base year could be set up on a fiscal year basis beginning July 1st, to coincide with property tax assessments.

The lease will define your premises as a percentage of the building area or of the project. This percentage is then applied to the increase over the base year or comparison year for operating expenses, taxes or other owner's costs are subject to escalation over the base year.

Sometimes it is possible to negotiate a cap on operating expense increases including taxes. The cap is usually expressed as a percentage such as 5% annually. In some states, like Georgia, property taxes can rise dramatically when a property is sold or transferred and a limit on the amount of taxes that can be passed through to you is very important, especially if the property has been held for a long time. While you may receive assurances that the owner has no intention of selling during your lease term, that is not enough, since people still die and the property may be transferred for estate planning purposes or by reason of death. If the owner says he has no intention of selling, then giving you a cap on tax increases should not be a problem.

Capital improvements to the property should either be excluded from the operating expense increases or amortized over their useful life and only that portion passed through annually. Always ask if there are capital improvements planned and how they will be treated in the lease. Be aware that common area refurbishment such as floor and wall coverings, elevator cab finishes, and other repairs are not usually considered capital improvements. If you are leasing a space in a building with tired common areas, a portion of the refurbishment could be billed to you after the base year has passed.

Note: Some smaller properties owned by individuals, will not want to go though all the calculations and ensuing discussions with tenants about these kinds of increases. Instead, they might simply ask for a flat percentage increase annually. While this is easier for both parties, typically this kind of increase is based upon the entire rental payment. Whereas, expense increases are only applied to that portion of the rent that goes to cover a particular expense. So you could pay more for this convenience.

RENEWAL OPTIONS

Typically, one of three methods of establishing the new rental rate is used. The **fixed rate option method** is the clearest and easiest to understand. Unfortunately, since each side of the transaction has a different forecast of future values, it is also frequently the most difficult one upon which to reach agreement.

The second method is a **Cost of Living Adjustment** and is based upon one of two Consumer Price Indexes. Either an index showing the increase in cost of living for all urban consumers in a particular area, or the index of all urban wage earners and clerical workers in the nation are used. The problem with this method is that the indexes do not bear much relation to the rental value of a particular property. Additionally, many lease agreements call for annual CPI adjustments during the lease term to prevent income erosion. As a result, an option to renew based upon a CPI increase is, in fact, an extension of the original lease without any real increase in rents.

Market rental value adjustments are more flexible and meet the needs of both owner and tenant. Several months before the lease expires, the tenant notifies the owner in writing of its desire to exercise the option. Within a specified time period, the parties endeavor to reach an agreement, if unable to reach an agreement, then each party hires a third party appraiser or qualified broker to establish the market value. Should the experts be unable to agree, then a third expert is usually hired to settle the issue. Some lease contracts also send the disputed estimates of value to Superior Court for final resolution. Because each of these methods is costly, frequently the parties reach agreement before resorting to hiring experts.

OPERATING HOURS OF THE BUILDING

Normally you will have access to your premises 7 days a week, 24 hours a day, 365 days a year. And you can expect that the electrical plugs and lights and elevators will be operating. Many of the other services that the owner is obligated to provide, such as heating ventilating and air conditioning (HVAC), guard services, building engineers, etc will only be available during the building operating hours. If you need to operate on an extended hour or 24/7 basis, the cost of providing you with these services will be charged to you, if they can be provided at all. This is a big issue for some properties and a footnote for others. In larger multi-tenant buildings it can be very costly to provide after-hours HVAC and require an engineer on site to do so. Other buildings are set up to provide these services at the flip of a switch in your premises, using computer billing. Many smaller properties have no problem with extended hour operations since the tenant is already paying for the services directly. If you need extended hours of operations, broach the subject with the owner and make sure the services you want can be delivered affordably before you get too far along in the transaction.

MAINTENANCE, REPAIRS, ALTERATIONS AND ADDITIONS

The lease will set out the obligations of the parties for maintenance and repairs of the premises and you must be sure that this accurately reflects your understanding. As a general rule, in a full service gross lease used in office space, or in any kind of lease covering multi-tenant property, the tenant will be responsible for the interior and owner for the exterior and common areas.

At a later date you might want to reconfigure your premises or do other remodeling work. This is always subject to the owner's prior written consent and approval. In highly controlled properties such as high rises or large shopping centers, expect this to be very restrictive as to what you can do, who can do the work, how and when the work can be done. In some cases you can negotiate to permit alterations up to a certain dollar amount without going through a consent process, and I suggest you do this whenever possible. This can be a great help if you need to sublet a portion of your premises or need an image makeover. You will be required to keep the property lien free.

At the end of the lease you will be required to return the premises in the same condition in which you received them, normal wear and tear expected. The owner may have the right to require you to restore the premises to its original configuration or remove your fixtures and equipment. Be sure to exclude any original tenant improvements from this requirement. Try to get the owner to waive any restoration rights for subsequent alterations at the time you make application for consent to alter the premises during the lease term. You will also need to remove the improvements before the lease expires or the owner could continue to charge you rent. If you wait to remove any improvements of fixtures that you are required to remove, you could be considered a hold over tenant and subject to substantial rent increases under the holding over provision of the lease.

INSURANCE ISSUES

Regardless of whether or not you are reimbursing the owner for their insurance policies, you will be required to provide your own insurance. Start by sending this part of the lease contract to your insurer along with any clauses that deal with attornment, indemnification and and/ or subrogation.

Some of the coverage you may be required to provide includes:

- Liability
- Casualty to tenant improvements
- Business or rent interruption
- Lost rental value
- Plate glass

Be aware that if your use of the premises increases the cost of coverage to the building, any adjacent premises, or common areas, that cost would most likely be passed on to you. After you have received assurances from your insurer that you can obtain the coverage required, discuss the ramifications of the indemnification, attornment and subrogation with your legal counsel.

ASSIGNMENT AND SUBLETTING

We've gone over some of the aspects of assignment and subletting and these clauses are becoming more and more restrictive. Be sure you know your rights and obligations as well as the rights retained by the owner. The owner will always require that they consent to any assignment or subletting.

The Key issues to look for are:

- Who is entitled to any bonus rent from the subletting?
- Does the owner have the right to terminate the lease or a portion of the lease in the event of a subletting?
- What are the rental rates you can advertise?
- How much time is the owner permitted to give or withhold consent?
- What are the legal fees charged by the owner in granting consent?

- What uses are restricted from subletting or assignment?

- Can the owner increase the rental rate to current market level in the event of sublease or assignment?

- What financial qualifications is the subtenant or assignee required to have?

Be aware that many options to expand or renew are personal to the original tenant and do not pass with an assignment or sublease.

EARLY TERMINATION RIGHTS

Sometimes tenants are concerned with outgrowing the space before the lease expires. Usually the solution is to sublet or assign the lease. However, if the sublease and assignment provisions are too restrictive, you may want to try to negotiate an early termination of the lease. There are costs associated with the right to terminate early. Normally, you will be expected to pay several months rent while the owner finds a substitute tenant. If the owner has provided substantial amounts of tenant improvements on your behalf, you must expect to repay the unamortized portion of the improvements. If a broker has been paid a commission, the early termination penalty may include repayment of a portion of that fee. While early termination penalties are expensive, for some tenants they are preferable to the position of being a sublessor and the potential liabilities of those duties.

RELOCATION WITHIN THE PROJECT

Another lease clause that can have serious economic consequences is the owner's right to relocate you within the complex. Owners need this in multi-tenant properties to allow them to plan for growth of superior tenants or properly plan shopping center. While you might have to live with such a clause in your lease, you may be able to provide yourself with some protections. First, the owner should pay for the cost of the relocation and improving the premises to a like condition as your original premises. However, there are a number of incidents such as reprinting stationery and brochures, telephone or other equipment relocations, and above-standard tenant improvements. How much notice you will be given to relocate is critical. If you need high speed Internet or other connectivity, you need to anticipate the lead-time required for installing those services. Ask for some cash compensation to cover the inconvenience and discourage relocation. Toward the end of your lease you might not want to be relocated so ask for the option to terminate the lease if relocation is required during the last year of the term.

HOLDING OVER

Holding over is another clause that can cause your rent expense to double. At the end of the term, the owner may need you to vacate on time to avoid delaying the possession by another tenant. To ensure that you do vacate on time, a provision is made in the lease that increases the rent if you stay beyond the lease term, without the owner's consent. This can be an increase of 115% to 200% of the base rent. If you obtain the owner's consent to stay, this will not be an issue. The lease will become a month-to-month tenancy and the owner can adjust the rent upon 30 days written notice.

LATE CHARGES AND INTEREST

The late charge is used to offset the costs incurred by the owner in collecting late rent and as a preventative measure against late rent. Most leases do provide a grace period, 3 to 5 days is typical. You can often negotiate 1 or 2 forgiveness' of late charges per year as this will probably save you more money if you forget to pay on time. The interest rate is for longer, incurred monetary defaults and is applied to those overdue amounts in addition to any late charges.

THE ENTIRE AGREEMENT

The balance of the lease must be reviewed by your legal counsel and discussed thoroughly to make sure you understand what you are signing. Do not get lulled into thinking that the bulk of the lease is boilerplate; you never know what may be buried in the miscellaneous provisions.

Most leases contain a provision stating that this is the entire agreement and that you have not relied upon any other representations and that there are no other outside agreements. To make sure this is accurate, review all your proposals and notes on the transaction and check to see everything you have been promised is in the lease.

CHAPTER 19

14 Negotiating Tips for Your Counter Offer

You should assume that you will get an unacceptable response back from the Landlord and many wonder what issues need to be countered. Well, the short answer is that everything that doesn't meet your <u>wants</u> should be counter offered. But below is a brief list of common sense items to consider when preparing to meet with the Landlord:

1. **Always ask for more than what you want and accept more that what you need.** I constantly see people who are hard negotiators in their own businesses forget what has gotten them to be great negotiators. You must ask for the stars and be willing to accept the moon.

2. **Demand lower rent! That's right, demand it.** Don't ask for it. If you have the market information that will support your rent requirements you will be in a stronger position to dictate to the Landlord what rent should be, not what he wants.

3. **Demand increased Tenant Improvement Allowances.** Again, market knowledge of what T.I. allowances are appropriate as well as what is the vacancy status with the Landlord will further support your demand for higher than offered allowances.

4. **Demand lower fixed escalations.** The effect of at least a 1% decrease in the fixed escalation requirement could mean the difference between hiring and not hiring an additional employee.

5. **Demand a Cap on Pass Thru Expenses.** Many competent leases may permit expenses above the base year amount of expenses to be passed thru to the Tenant. First, attempt to eliminate this clause as you are already paying escalations. But, secondly, if you can't eliminate this, limit the amount above the base year's expense amount to a mere 10% of the total increase. This will limit how much they can pass on to your business.

6. **Demand Free Rent.** Landlords, depending on their vacancy and economic status may be more or less receptive to free rent. Too bad. Ask for as much free rent as you are aware of in the market for similar situated properties and then ask for more than that. You may be surprised at what the Landlord may give you.

7. **Demand Reduced, Late and Holdover Fees.** Late rental payments can be 10% of your monthly rental. Holdover fees for Tenants who are moving out of the space, but may require staying beyond the end of the term of the lease, may equate to 200% of the rental rate. It is not your intention to pay late or to stay beyond the terms of the original lease but, things

happen. Using a rental figure of $6000.00 per month, that can equate to $600.00 in late fees and $12,000.00 a month in holdover rent. Lowering these rates to 5% for late fees and 125% for holdover rental rates will save your business $300.00 and $4500.00 respectively.

8. **Demand Moving Expenses.** Why not. The cost of a move can range between $2000.00 -$100,000.00 depending upon the size and complexity of the move. Why not ask for this? If you have done your research on the market conditions, the landlord may be more than excited to get a new Tenant in his building and having him pay for your moving expenses will give the Landlord the edge that you need to sign his lease.

9. **Read the Lease.** Earlier in this chapter I invited you to have your broker and/or legal counsel assist you with the lease. I did not tell you to rely solely on their advice. You need to read and re-read the lease to make sure you understand what you are being asked to do and that the terms you've discussed are part of the document.

10. **Understand the Terms within the Lease.** It is not just an issue to read the lease; it is paramount that you have a keen understanding of the terminology associated with the lease. (Negotiating tip: It is important to understand the difference between the words may and shall. May means that the landlord has the option to do something at their leisure. Shall means that the Landlord must do something by a prescribed time.)

11. **Negotiate Out Clauses.** Unless you have a working crystal ball, it is difficult to project with 100% certainty what will happen with your business. You need to provide yourself

the flexibility to terminate the lease early if (hopefully) you outgrow the premises before the end of the lease. Usually this will require some notice to the landlord and an early termination fee. But these requirements are easier to deal with as opposed to cramming people into a space that is ill equipped for your business' growth for the remaining 3 years of your lease.

12. **Negotiate Default Language.** Like the late fees, you are not going into a lease with the idea that you will default on your lease but, if the working crystal ball is off, your business may run into cash flow problems from time to time that may affect your ability to pay rent. Having a solid understanding of the repercussions of the default language entails and minimizing objectionable language that will provide clarity for your business and easier methods to cure default. Remember, the language in the entire lease is written in favor of the Landlord so anything you can do to counter that language will be in your best interest.

13. **Negotiate Extensions.** As shown in the Chapter 15, the proposal is the first area where you can begin the discussion on extensions. Dictate to the Landlord what you want in this arena.

14. **Negotiate Insurance Requirements.** Every lease will have different requirements to fulfill the Landlord's or more often then not, the Landlord's bank's insurance needs. Some owners will do all they can to have so much insurance that you essentially replace the office building in the event of a loss. Others are more reasonable. You may want to contact your insurance agent to discuss what you will be willing

to do. A broker should know what level of insurance the market typically requires.

Now that you have some cannon fodder for you to go after the offers and the lease, it is important to have a better understanding of the art of the negotiation.

CHAPTER 20

Negotiating Strategies

Now let's talk about negotiation. First, whether or not you like to negotiate is irrelevant. You must learn to negotiate because you are going to encounter top negotiators who will take you to the cleaners if you don't recognize and know how to counter what they are doing. These top negotiators sometimes include owners and their brokers. And, they'll use negotiating techniques on you to get what they want. Therefore it is critical to learn how to negotiate.

If it's not the most comfortable thing in the world for you to negotiate then let me offer you this, think of negotiating as a game. In a game you are seeking to win, because winning is the object, but you are not overly concerned about losing. In other words, the best negotiators don't let emotions, such as stress, dictate the outcome of a negotiation because it's simply a game that they are playing. This is easier if you are not tied to the outcome. In other words, if you can resign yourself to walk away if you have to, you'll be much more apt to treat the negotiation as a game and you'll be more effective. If you maintain this attitude, you'll be able to feel excited about the negotiating process.

So let me share with you some thoughts about negotiations, and then I'll walk you through some of the techniques you might encounter in the process of negotiating. As with all techniques, you don't necessarily have to use them to get what you want, and that's your decision, but you better know when they are being used on you, and the counter measures necessary to be an effective negotiator.

So what's the process of negotiating? Well, every negotiation is different but some general rules apply.

3 RULES FOR SUCCESSFUL NEGOTIATIONS

RULE #1: My first rule of negotiation is to avoid over negotiating. After all, when it comes to real estate, it's all negotiable! Virtually every aspect of a lease transaction is negotiable but that doesn't mean you should negotiate every point. A common mistake is over negotiating. Overkill on minor points is an error that can evoke feelings of frustration, anger and resentment in the other party. When the "romance goes out of the deal" it is usually attributed to over negotiating.

RULE #2: The 2nd rule is to prepare. Since there are thousands of variations of lease clauses that need to be combined with the economic variables of the transaction, it is important to reach agreement on all the key issues early in the process. Structure your lease negotiations into 2 components,

- the general business terms
- the lease language review

Proper Preparation Prevents Poor Performance. Successful negotiators take the time to prepare before they enter the negotiating arena.

Develop an agenda of deal points you wish to cover. Start with those points that can be readily agreed upon. As you work toward the more difficult issues you can reference all the prior points of agreement to help you get through impasses. Decide in advance how far you will bend on the business terms and stick to those limits.

RULE #3: My 3rd rule is to meet in person with all parties involved whenever possible. Negotiating the lease language can be left to the attorneys but you run the risk of losing control of the negotiation and it can be expensive. It's almost always better to take the attorney's comments directly to the table yourself. Taking the time to understand these points will allow you to pare down the list in advance, eliminating small or inconsequential items.

I like to negotiate in person as much as possible. Unfortunately we are not always afforded the opportunity or have the necessary time to meet in person. We often find ourselves in a position of negotiating over the phone. Miscommunications occur far too easily on the phone because we cannot see the other person's nonverbal communications and signals. It is also much easier to say no over the phone than it is in person.

Fortunately, we can strengthen our position substantially when time or distance forces us to use the phone to negotiate, as with any negotiation the preparation of your position and establishment of the limits of your concessions are important to your success. Take the time to commit your position in writing and fax or email it before your phone call to clarify and strengthen your position. Turf exists, even on the phone. Make sure that you place the call to ensure that you are working from your agenda, following your order of events and concluding the call when you want.

Your body language as you speak on the phone is important. Have you ever had the feeling when talking with someone on the phone that they were leaning way back in their chair, perhaps barely listening, in a very relaxed position? So too is your body position transmitted through your voice. I think the best body position is standing; yet relaxed and smiling as you speak. This conveys the message that you are interested and alert. If you get too laid back or relaxed, you may find yourself making too many concessions, too quickly. Standing up to make important calls is a must and my office is set up to do that, I use a headset and I have a desktop lectern for taking notes. Note taking is a listening technique that is highly relevant in negotiations. To close a telephone negotiation with the clearest possible communication, verbally summarize your conversation. After the call, your notes can be very valuable to confirm your understanding with the other party. Immediately fax or email your notes including a summary of your understanding to avoid problems later.

This is so important that I'll say it again; written preparation and strong communication skills can help overcome the inherent disadvantages of negotiating over the telephone. Use faxes or email to employ the power of the written word and strengthen your position. Watch your body language, smile as you speak, fax or email copies of your notes for clarity and you will be doing a superior job for yourself.

Next, set time limits for each negotiating session to help avoid deadlocks and prevent over negotiating. If you need to stage your negotiations into 2 or 3 sessions, then prepare your presentation of the essential points in advance. One way to do this is, if you have many minor lease comments, to set up a separate meeting to work on these after agreement has been reached on the business terms. Once you begin your meeting, remember that rapport is important in any negotiation, and so spend the first few moments establishing rapport. Once you have the rapport you need to boldly ask for what you want, usually one thing at a time. You need to keep asking until you have everything you want or until it becomes apparent that the other side is not willing to concede on an item. Skilled negotiators are trained to ask, and ask again. So develop many ways to ask.

If the other side is skilled at asking for what they want, they will ask until they get exactly that! It is important to develop at least 10 ways to say NO to this type of negotiator. This takes practice and discipline but you can master this technique if you are prepared to walk away from any deal. If you have to have the deal, the other party need only wait you out to win. The appearance that you are prepared to leave the deal can neutralize the pressure to say yes.

Next you need to know how to make concessions. Concession patterns are often detectable in the other party's negotiating style and by getting to know as much as possible about the other party you can gain the advantage. Test for a concession pattern by bringing several minor issues to the table early in the session.

- **Does the other party like to dispose of the issues quickly?** The negotiator that likes to dispose of one issue in order to get to the next one may tend to give up too much too soon.

- **Does the other party like to take a long time to consider the issues?** Putting too much time pressure on this individual may cause them to walk away.

- **Do they attempt to extract concession for concession?** If so, bunch several demands together to minimize your concessions.

Testing the other party for style and patterns helps you see how far they will go to make a deal. Likewise, make sure your concession patterns are not too easily detected. Develop a habit of giving in slowly to the other party's demands. It is easy to fall into the trap of conceding to create an irregular pattern. Make minor concessions to gain the concessions that are most important to you.

If you start to feel trapped into making concessions that you don't want, there are several ways out. You can invoke the absent authority, citing the need to consult with another decision-maker, or you can declare a time out to consider a counter offer. Break off the negotiation smoothly by setting a time to meet again, using the time to plan for a new session. Also, be aware when others are using the absent authority on you.

If the other party makes an outrageous demand, it may be their way of testing your resolve to make the deal. If you are committed to make the deal you may find yourself considering those concessions that were out of the question before. If you are the recipient of such a demand try these 3 defenses.

1. Ignore the demand until it has been raised for the second or third time.

2. Laugh it off and tell them they can't be serious or use the walk away.

3. Observe concession patterns and the negotiating style of the other party.

Give in slowly. Learn to say NO. Be prepared to walk away from any deal by having an acceptable back up location. It helps to be aware that an outrageous demand may be a test of your resolve. During your negotiations take the time to write down every agreed upon point. Do it as the point is agreed upon. This adds a feeling of certainty to what has been agreed upon and prevents the other side from going back on something that has already been agreed upon. It also allows you to wrap up the negotiation by going over each point that you have written down, and then if necessary, have each party initial what has been written. While the initials do not constitute a legally binding agreement, they help to provide closure.

These are some of the most common negotiation techniques you will encounter, but the real lesson here is, that you will run into highly skilled negotiators and you must be prepared. By learning these techniques and others, you'll avoid serious gaffs in negotiations and show yourself to be a worthy negotiator.

CHAPTER 21

7 Critical Negotiating Techniques

There are 7 major techniques that you should recognize in a negotiation. They are:

1. The walk away

2. The absent authority

3. Deadlines

4. Nibbling

5. Grinding

6. Reframing questions

7. Controlled emotion

THE WALK AWAY

One of the simplest techniques that is employed in negotiating is the walk away. It is simply what the name implies. One party gets up and walks away from the deal. Not because they don't want the deal, but because they want to test the resolve of the other side. It is also important to understand that it may backfire. It is kind of like bluffing in poker. They may call your bluff. So in order to employ this technique it is important to be serious about letting the deal go if you have to, which goes back to the attitude that we talked about earlier. The best result of a walk away is that the other side calls you back to make the concession that you walked away about. If someone walks out on you, you need to know how important each concession is and be willing to call someone back if you are willing to give in. Don't just give in when you call them back though. Call them back by saying that you will concede on this issue if they will concede on another. This lets them know that you want to continue, but that you are also not a push over. When the other side walks away, it can sometimes be a great time to ask for significant concessions because they may be looking for a way to come back. They may have bluffed and could be hoping that you don't call it.

THE ABSENT AUTHORITY

This is a common and powerful technique that allows you to slow down making concessions and many times eliminates the request for concessions from the other side. It is simply the technique of telling the other side that there is someone that you need to get approval from. If you find this technique being used by the other side, then simply request to know the authorities opinion on something before making a concession. In other words say, "I'll consider that if I know for sure that your associate will agree to it." This will kill their attempts to pin you down and cause them to either get approval or admit that it is not that important.

DEADLINES

When you set the deadline you control the negotiation. Because approximately 80% of the agreements are reached in the last 20% of the negotiation, it is important to understand that the person who sets the deadline manages this aspect of the negotiation. And be aware when others invoke deadlines. As your deadline approaches, the more likely it is that the other party will concede to your demands. Combine the power of competition with your deadline to increase your effectiveness. Suppose that in negotiating these terms I say, "It's been yours and one other property." If we are apart on an economic issue, I can say that I want to give this further consideration. "I'll give you my final determination on Friday", if they want to wrap up the deal sooner, they may need to make some additional concessions.

Always test the other party's deadline. When the other party is attempting to set the deadlines, it is important to question their deadlines. If they say to you, "I need your answer by Friday morning", don't acquiesce without finding out why. Good responses to this statement would be: "Why Friday?" or "Do you have another prospective transaction for this space?" If they answer "yes" to this last question asked, "How long have you been working with them?" or "How far along are you in that deal?" Dig into this issue to test its veracity. The more you question, the better your chances are of eliciting responses that will restore the negotiating to you.

When you set the deadline you have the power to change it. Extending a deadline is a delicate aspect of the negotiating process. It is a technique that can be used to your advantage, but it should be used infrequently. Continually extending deadlines can be misconstrued. If you call me on Friday and ask "What is your decision?" I would probably respond by asking you about a deal point I want a concession on. If you decline to concede this point I may consider re-establishing my deadline to allow you time to reconsider. I might say, "I haven't had the time to reach my decision yet. However, unless you can meet my needs by Wednesday I'll probably take another property. How about calling me back Wednesday or sooner if you change your mind?" The key here is to recognize the other party's attempts to control the deadline and to establish your own deadlines.

NIBBLING

Nibbling is asking for additional concessions after agreement. It uses the concept of commitment and consistency. Whether you choose to use nibbling in your negotiations is a personal decision, nevertheless, you should know about nibbling. The most common form of nibbling occurs when you have just made a major decision for example, to buy a car. After you have made your deal, the car dealer offers to sell you an array of options. The dealer knows that you are most susceptible to buying these items immediately after making the big decision. These items are loaded with profit for the dealer. The selling or negotiating that goes on just after sale or agreement has been reached is called nibbling.

There is tremendous tension during the negotiations for both parties. That tension is released when the agreement is reached and both parties feel a great sense of relief at the moment of agreement. This is when the nibbler casually presents one or two additional requests. Often they are couched in an assumptive closing statement. The other party, not wanting to reopen the negotiation and risk losing the deal quietly goes along.

The primary defense against nibbling is to make the nibbler feel cheap. Another defense is to offer to re-open the negotiation.

Remember that the other party feels the pressure too and probably is not inclined to re-open the negotiation. Another way to defend yourself against a nibbler is to invoke the absent authority, simply defer the decision to them. Often the nibble will be withdrawn at this point. It will be easier to say no to a nibble when the glow of a successful negotiation has faded. Remember that at the moment of agreement you and the other party are both susceptible to give up additional concessions. Prepare your defenses against nibbling in advance and anticipate that they may come.

GRINDING AWAY

Have you ever felt as though the other party will never stop coming back for more during a negotiation? That each time you get close to agreement the other party makes additional demands? That they are grinding away and you are powerless to stop them? This is known as grinding and there are several good defenses against the grinding away process. Always ask something in return for each concession you make. This is called trading off and it is important to a successful negotiation because it creates value in the concessions you are making. No matter how inconsequential the concession may seem to you, develop the practice of asking for something in return. In developing this practice know that timing is important. Take time to consider carefully the other party's demands to avoid responding too quickly. Overly quick responses tend to send the message that you don't take the demands seriously or that you are trying to shift away attention from the issue.

There is a principle that says that the value of services is greatly diminished after the services have been rendered. For this reason it is better to ask for a trade off when you make your response rather than save it for later. However, if you have established value in your concessions by asking for something in return, even if you don't get it, you can say "We did that for you back then, now we want you to do this for us."

Withdraw a prior concession to send a strong bottom line message. Grinders need to be told when to stop. When you take something back that you have previously given up you are sending a bottom line message that says, "We have gone as far as we will go and if you keep asking for more, we will need something back."

RE-FRAMING QUESTIONS

A Re-framing question is a technique that some negotiators use to redirect or change the original focus. This technique is a valuable one to both who use and recognize a re-framing question. In a negotiation pay close attention for subtle re-framing sentences like "I think the question we need to ask here is…" Chances are they are about to attempt a reframe. The way to counteract this is to listen carefully to what is being said. Do not agree with it if it does not focus the negotiation on the points that you need to focus on.

CONTROLLED EMOTION

There are negotiators that have mastered the use of controlled emotion as a negotiating tactic. The most recognizable are flinching, showing anger and the walking away.

Have you ever been in a situation where after quoting your asking price the other party physically flinches and says, "I had no idea you were asking that much! I'll never pay that price!" If you reacted by lowering your price or offering some other concession, you probably fell prey to the flinch. To defend against the flinch you must first recognize it for what it is. Flinching is both an opening gambit designed to lower your expectations and more important, it is an expression of interest. Respond calmly; imply flexibility without making a specific concession, then turn the discussion to the benefits of your tenancy. Attempt to get the other party to make the first offer, to establish the bottom of the settlement range.

Sadly, some people still use anger to gain concessions in a negotiation. This tactic is designed to get you to deal with the other party's emotions rather than the issues. We often find this tactic tied to the walk away. The best defense is to focus your attention on the movement of the goal concessions as they cross the table. Keep your attention on what is going on with issues and not what the people are doing in the negotiations.

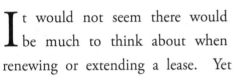

CHAPTER 22

Renewing or Extending a Lease

It would not seem there would be much to think about when renewing or extending a lease. Yet there are some costly and common mistakes. One of the most common mistakes is simply exercising an option to renew when market conditions favor the tenant. Some others include:

- Waiting too long to renew the lease

- Obtaining information about market conditions from the owner

- Failing to establish a new base year

- Not renegotiating a security deposit

- Failing to obtain a refurbishment allowance

- Not creating a verifiable sense of competition with the owner to retain you as a tenant

When market conditions favor the tenant, it may be far better to renegotiate the basic business terms than to simply renew. I always recommend that the tenant take a good look at what the market has to offer 6 months before the end of the lease term or before exercising an option to renew. If you use a broker to do this, be careful not to abuse their time. If you end up moving, the broker will get paid, but if you stay put they may not. I suggest you work out consolation compensation if you do not relocate. You would not appreciate having your time wasted and being used as a free source of market information about your business, and brokers are no different. You can also make an exclusive tenant representation agreement with a broker, who can then be paid by the owner to represent you in the renewal as well as to the open market. Since this does create a verifiable sense of needing to compete to retain you as a tenant, you can benefit greatly from this action.

As you are approaching the end of a lease term, the most common mistake is waiting too long to open discussions about renewing. Begin the negotiations early enough to allow you time to relocate if the transaction fails to reach satisfactory terms. It is clearly in the owner's best interests to delay reaching agreement until time is too short for you to relocate before your lease expires. This kind of pressure on a tenant can be costly. Start your renewal discussions early and set and control the deadlines for response. If your deadlines are not met, begin looking for a new location and let it be known that you are looking around.

In the section on letters of intent and again in the section on understanding lease clauses we talked about how rental rates are established upon exercising an option to renew. The renewal rate would either be; a fixed rate increase, a CPI increase, fair market value or a percentage of fair market value (F.M.V.). If rental rates have not risen to the level of a previously negotiated fixed rate increase, then a re-negotiation is essential to avoid overpaying. While a CPI index is commonly used to establish future rental rates, it bears little relationship to commercial property rental rates. Such renewal options contain a statement that the renewal rate shall not be less than the last rent in effect at the time of renewal, which can cause the renewal to be at over-market rates. If the escalated rent is above market then a re-negotiation is required.

If the renewal option is fair market value, or a discounted percentage of F.M.V. then the vital task is to understand the market. This includes any inducements to leases being offered to new tenants coming into the property, which otherwise may not be calculated into a renewal option by the owner. Do not rely upon the owner to provide you with this information.

Now let's take a look at what is at stake for the owner if you move out. In a soft market it might take several months to locate and successfully negotiate a lease with a new tenant after you vacate. The owner is likely to have to provide tenant improvements for the new tenant. (This can range from just paint and carpet upgrades to extensive renovations, costing from $5 to $20 per square foot.) There are the hard costs of renovation, such as the contractors' work, and the soft costs such as the architectural and engineering, permits and supervision. No rent is collected during the construction period. Additionally, the owner might have to offer free rent or a graduated rent schedule to procure a tenant. In very soft markets, moving allowances are offered as a lease enticement. The owner may incur additional legal fees to prepare, review and negotiate the lease contract. These costs can become quite significant.

On your side of the equation, there are the moving expenses and the disruption to your business to consider, but if the market favors the tenant, take the time to learn the market and renegotiate rather than renew and ask for some of the concessions covered here. You may be successful in obtaining a refurbishment of the premises, a rent holiday or period or reduced rent as well as ensuring that your rental rate is truly market rate.

If you have been faithful in your performance of the lease obligations, then a return of your security deposit is in order. Security deposits do not typically earn interest for you, and over a ten-year term you'd be surprised at how much that can cost you. A $5,000 deposit earning 6% interest, compounded monthly, is worth $6,744 after just 5 years. Not that much you say, but after ten years it grows to $9,096, nearly double! So get that security deposit back if you can!

A very costly mistake is failing to establish a new base year. Most renewal options do not reestablish the base year as the renewal year. Therefore, all the increases in operating expenses, taxes and insurance are then compared to the original year of the lease. All of the escalation that has accumulated over the previous years of the lease term remains in effect for the renewal period. By establishing a new base year, those are washed away and for the first year of the new term, you will be relieved of the obligation to pay any operating expense pass-trough's.

Again, decide early whether you are going to simply exercise a renewal option or re-negotiate your lease. Then study the market and control the deadlines to avoid being rushed into less than favorable renewal terms.

CHAPTER 23

Lease Execution

So now it's time to get the lease signed and hopefully all your hard work will pay off with the granting of an interest in real property by the owner. You will be required to sign up to 4 copies of the lease in original signature. I suggest you initial every page of the lease when you are signing to prevent any accidental substitution of pages. Next you need to provide good funds to cover the first month's rent and any security deposits, or contribution to tenant improvements. You also need to deliver an insurance binder from your insurer.

The lease is not a contract until the owner has signed and delivered it back to you and, up until that point, the deal may be terminated by either party. This does not happen often but if it happens to you, see your attorney as you might have a cause of action against the owner.

After the lease is delivered to you, the parties' obligations begin.

IT'S TIME TO START CONSTRUCTION!!

If the owner is responsible for constructing the premises for you, the working drawings will commence at this time. During the working drawing stage, you will have certain obligations to approve the designs, provide information about furnishing or fixtures, select finishes and the like. Be sure to calendar the critical dates so that you are not the cause of any delays in completing the work. Delays caused by tenants can cause the rent to start even though the space has not been completed and delivered to you. Once the work starts be sure to schedule your cabling, equipment and furniture installers with the contractor or project manager to ensure a smooth transition into the building and an undisputed commencement date. Once you've moved in be sure to execute a notice of lease term commencement with the owner.

STAGE V

2-1 MONTHS AWAY: Construction Stage

We are nearing the end of the leasing process but it's not over yet! Many people feel that the office leasing process ends once the signed lease is delivered and unfortunately this is where many brokers experience ends. But the Construction stage is one of the most critical stages of the leasing process. This is the point that your new "home" is being built. Money is being spent and often it is your money. Selections need to be made and a schedule needs to be met! Depending on the business that you are in or the level of experience you have had with construction this may be review for you but it would be wise to have some good consultants during this process.

CHAPTER 24

Take Control of the Construction Process

The key element of the construction process is in the area of control. Most tenants don't take control because the either don't take the time, or have knowledge as to what actually goes into the building of their office space. They simply rely on the Landlord to do all of the work and accept what they get when it is all said and done. I have often wondered why this is the case. When you consider that, in today's work environment, you and your employees will spend as many or more time in their office space than they will in their own bedrooms, I question why people don't spend the same amount of time and effort as they do into the construction of their own homes. You are making an investment in both properties so why not have both locations live up to your standards…and not the Landlord's.

A client once asked me "How do you gain this control? After all, it's the Landlord's building and they should have the right to do whatever they want to make sure that their property meets their standards…" I told him that it was that sort of thinking that lead him to me. You need to work with the idea that the space is your space. As will be discussed ahead, interview and spend time to hire the architect. Take control of the contractor and construction process by making decisions with the help of the Landlord as to who will do the build-out and the scheduling that they must maintain to meet your needs. Much has been discussed in this book, that you must dictate the level of work that you want, how you want it to be done and when you want it to be done. Otherwise, you are going to be forced to settle for less. The first part in this process usually begins within the realm of the Architect/ Space Planner.

THE SPACE PLANNING PROCESS

Space planning usually occurs after an initial proposal has been tendered, although sometimes it will be delayed until the major deal points have been agreed upon and your credit reviewed. The proposals are conditioned upon reaching a mutually satisfactory space plan and a review of the associated costs.

Whether you will need space planning services or not will depend on the size of your transaction and the need to customize the location to meet your needs. If there will be construction, no matter how seemingly simple, the services of a qualified professional are essential, not optional. Because all construction requires building permits, and permits trigger inspections, it is possible that inspections could uncover required code corrections. Using a qualified architect will alert you to potential problems before you sign a lease. If you're in a tight market or responsible for the work of improvement for any reason, you do not want any surprises. Avoid unhappy surprises and use a qualified space planner when modifications are needed.

Larger office buildings often have space planners on retainer and offer their services to prospective tenants. Some will require that prospective tenants use the building architect. A commercial tenant requiring a substantial amount of office space is well advised to consider retaining his or her own architect. While building owners typically retain their own architects as an accommodation to prospective tenants, there are several good reasons to hire your own architect. First, due to the complex nature of today's office environment, including furniture systems, filing systems, computers and peripherals, your architect will understand your needs best. Additionally, as you narrow down your selection of properties, your architect is your best sounding board for efficiency, functionality and workflow.

Because building owners have budgeted for architect design services, in a softer market you can be successful in negotiating to have your architect's fees paid as part of the tenant's improvement allowance.

When I've seen problems arise in transactions that are centered on space planning issues, it's been because the architect selected to do the space planning has not been currently working with commercial property. Commercial interior space planning is relatively easy and any qualified architect can readily do preliminary plans. Where the problems arise is in underestimating the cost of commercial renovations, lack of knowledge about code issues and consequently using an approach to the job that results in over-designing the space. Stick with a specialist here and you'll avoid problems.

Again, space planning is usually done after the basic business terms are aligned and is normally a two to three week process to arrive at a satisfactory preliminary plan. This means that a set of drawings have been formulated and reviewed and are suitable for obtaining preliminary estimates from the contractors. Depending on the scope of work, allow about one to two weeks to complete the estimating. At the first meeting with the architect you will be conveying your requirements and desires. The architect develops the first plan, submits it to both the landlord and you for review and comments, and then makes the required revisions.

Another important step will be a technical review of the building being considered. This review is actually in two parts, the first of which will have been completed during the tours of the most qualified sites. At this time, you will need to review conditions in the building, which can affect the functional viability of the space (e.g. air conditioning, elevator size).

An architect or space planner should complete the second and more thorough step of the technical review. If you are using the building's architect, be sure to ask if there is code or functional issues with the building that might increase costs. Some areas of concern include potential problems with the interior construction, the life safety systems, the presence of asbestos, compliance with the ADA, energy conservation compliance, or other issues critical to the quality of your occupancy.

Here is another checklist for you to use with an architect. Be sure to discuss these items to avoid unhappy surprises later.

ARCHITECTUAL REVIEW CHECKLIST

- Review interior standards for sufficiency and quality
    - Partitions, Doors, Closets, Floor Coverings, Lighting Fixtures, Wall Finishes, Ceiling Tiles, Electrical Switches, Electrical Outlets, Telephone Outlets, H.V.A.C., Window Treatments, Life Safety Systems, Drinking Fountains
- Substantiate the dollar value of tenant work letter

- Review the policy on credits and substitutions of materials
- Estimate and review costs of over standard tenant improvements

REVIEW BUILDING SYSTEMS

- H.V.A.C
  - Machines for compression and pumping systems
  - Heat recovery and heat exchange
  - Air handling equipment, location and space
  - Number of zones per floor
  - After-hours procedures
- Power, Data, and Telecommunications
  - Service Capacity
  - Distribution method
  - Emergency generation
  - Power in watts/square foot
  - Lighting in watts/square foot
  - Telephone switching equipment
  - Satellite communications or microwave link
  - Shared tenant services
- Basic passenger service
  - Rentable square foot per elevator
  - Passenger weight capacity
  - Lighting controls
  - Service intervals

- Tenant lighting services
  - Switching capabilities
  - Fixture and lens type
  - Fixture and floor area ratio
- Lighting controls
- Freight
  - Dock ramps and levelers
  - Freight elevator specifications
- Ceiling and floor systems
  - Suspended ceiling components
  - Raised floor access potential
  - Poke-through potential
  - Services conveyed through ceiling or floor spaces
- Life safety and Security
  - Strobes
  - Sprinklers
  - Detection
  - Communication system
  - Loading dock security
- Building management systems
  - Building management systems and central controls
  - Master H.V.A.C. controls

CHAPTER 25

Construction Begins

N ow that you, the Landlord and the architect have reviewed and approved the plans for your new or remodeled office space, the real fun begins. The contractor who will perform the work is usually provided by the Landlord or may even be the Landlord. Neither of these scenarios is overly objectionable but, you will want to meet with the contractor before work begins to make sure that you are comfortable with their work. You will need to see examples of their work and ask them probing questions that will help you get an idea of the level of competence, skill and workmanship that they take with their projects. Find out if they have done work for the Landlord in the past and if so, where and when. If the construction was done in the building, take a look at the space with the contractor, or their employees to find things that you would like to correct and how they address items that need to be corrected. If the contractor is the Landlord, obviously you will be able to see what type of work they have done within the building itself.

It is not to say that you can't use a contractor of your choosing. I have done deals for clients who had experience with a contractor other than the Landlord's and the process went very well for both my client and the Landlord because the client was already comfortable with the level of workmanship that the contractor has performed. By taking control of this process, you will dictate to the Landlord what you require…not accept what they will give you.

After interviewing the contractors and finally agreeing to use one contractor agreeable to both the Landlord and, more importantly, to you, it is time to start mapping out a plan, a timeline to be exact of what will be done and when it will be completed by. Much in the same way that this book dispels what items need to be done and by what date they need to be done by, you should require that the contractor provide you a timeline with deadline dates for all stages of the improvement process. From permitting to the certificate of occupancy, your landlord and/or the contractor should be able to provide you a schedule similar to the one shown here.

As you can see, every aspect of the build-out process can easily be identified and can be referenced by anyone as to what should be happening and when. This will allow you to hold the contractors feet to the fire to ensure that you will be able to plan when your vendors can gain access and when you can move into your new or remodeled space.

Sometimes creating a schedule is not enough incentive for the contractor to get the project done in time. Get the Landlord to institute penalties, payable to your company, with the contractor if landmarks are not met. You may be ending your lease at your present location and may have a holdover rate that is two times the amount of the base rent. If these scheduled dates are not met, you may be forced to stay in your existing space beyond the termination and be subject to that higher rate. If you are not the cause of any delays, the contractor and/or the Landlord should be liable for paying any overage. Now you and the contractor are ready to get the construction underway.

It is important to get a few important issues out in the open. Don't get in the way of the contractor. You've gone to great lengths to meet, see and review with the contractor as to what you expect from him. You will want to make unannounced visits from time to time to make sure that what has been drawn is being built or that he is using the materials that you specified in the work-letter. But the worst thing you can do is to be onsite everyday watching the construction, getting involved with the contractors or their sub-contractors or constantly making changes. That having been said, I do recommend that you have some sort of regularly scheduled contact with the contractor. Whether it is by telephone or on site, schedule time to visit with the contractor. Remember, you will be living with this space for the next 5 years so you had better make sure that it turns out right from the beginning. This meeting should take no longer than fifteen minutes and simply involve checking on the schedule. This issue of timing becomes very important when it comes to the issue of vendors.

CHAPTER 26

Vendor Coordination

You're not done yet. There are several items which still must be done during the construction process that is your responsibility and the earlier you respond to these items the better opportunity you will have to get them completed before it is time to move into your space. For example, does your business use telephones? If you've tried to get new service in any office market around the country today, it is not a 2 day process anymore. Often, it can take up to 10 weeks between the initial call to the Telephone Company and final installation of the service. Another issue is that of moving. I am constantly amazed at the number of people who wait until the last week to try and schedule a moving company and are dismayed that no reputable company has the time to move them. These otherwise organized business people wind up using Johnny Six-pack and his Merry Movers. Those items which actually complete the move from the old space to the new premises are damaged. Develop a vendor checklist to provide you a method of clearing vendor issues that need to be attended to before commencement day.

CHAPTER 27

The Final Walk-Thru: It's Moving Day

It's crunch time as decisions impacting your forthcoming move are being made with great pace. You've followed the numerous guidelines offered to you in this book and you now have about two weeks left before it is commencement date. The construction appears to be starting to come together. At this stage in the game, I would suggest that you set a meeting date with the construction people two weeks prior to your move in date to have an open, honest discussion about the schedule and any possible problems which may delay your moving into the space. This will let you know where you stand and what adjustments you may need to make.

Just prior to your moving into the space, do a walk thru with the construction personnel and/or building manager to identify defects in the workmanship or the products that simply do not work. Light switches not working the right lights, HVAC ducts not functioning correctly, and walls showing they were not properly painted are but a few of the numerous yet common re-work items that are often identified on a punch list. The Move-In Inspection (located in the Appendix) will identify many of the issue that you need to be comfortable with in order to make sure that you get the office space you are paying for.

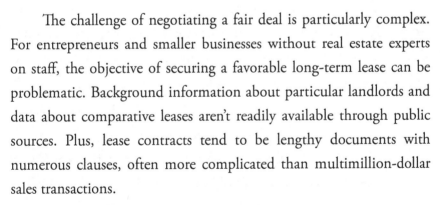

CHAPTER 28

Congratulations–
You're Home

Real estate is always about location, location, location and that holds true when it comes to buying property...but when negotiating a commercial real estate lease there are many other factors to consider.

The challenge of negotiating a fair deal is particularly complex. For entrepreneurs and smaller businesses without real estate experts on staff, the objective of securing a favorable long-term lease can be problematic. Background information about particular landlords and data about comparative leases aren't readily available through public sources. Plus, lease contracts tend to be lengthy documents with numerous clauses, often more complicated than multimillion-dollar sales transactions.

While most people tend to focus on the economic aspects of leasing it is equally important to focus on non-economic issues. Options to expand, options to renew and options to cancel are all things to consider and negotiate. In fact, the structure of the deal often proves to be the most crucial financial component. Many people think that if the square footage costs are good that they should lock in a long-term deal. But the savings might not add up in the long term if the business flounders. In some cases it's better for new enterprises or businesses that are weathering the recession to pay a little higher rate to retain flexibility rights.

A LEASE is like a marriage, and a SALE is like a divorce...Thus, once the sale is completed, it's over. But when all the negotiations, contracts and construction are completed... tenants and landlords are partnered together and depend on each other for success for years and years. And just as a Successful Marriage...it is critical when it comes to negotiating a lease...it's got to be a win-win for both tenants and landlords.

If a Landlord takes advantage of a Tenant in the lease negotiations...the resentment will linger for the term of the lease, which typically leads to tenants moving out at the end of their lease. On the other hand if a Tenant sticks it to the Landlord during the negotiations... the Landlord will follow "the letter of the lease" but nothing extra. And as soon as the tenant needs some help or wants something extra, the Landlord will use that opportunity to get revenge for the original lease negotiations.

This is important to keep in mind because in the "leasing game" there are no winners and losers...either everyone is a WINNER or everyone is a LOSER. If you use the strategies and tactics that I teach in this book to beat your Landlord into submission (and if you follow my advice you can!) then you can count on some resentment coming back to you...and it usually comes when you can lease afford it. Just as the market is really soft now, it may be very tight five years from now. You need to maintain a good relationship with your landlord.

If you've made it this far in the book, I believe you will be better prepared to lease a commercial office space than many of the clients I have been privileged to have served over the past two decades. Whether or not you choose to use a broker is up to you, but by being well informed about leasing office properties you will be well armed, and that will make all the difference to you and your business during your next lease negotiation.

Appendix

GLOSSARY OF COMMON LEASING TERMS

FORMS

- Space Needs Worksheet
- Site Tour Rating Form
- Office Space Rating Survey
- Proposal Evaluation Form
- Summary of Proposal Form
- Lease Summary Sheet
- Building Information Form
- Move-In Checklist

FREE LEASE PROPOSAL EVALUATION CONSULTATION

WHAT IS THE PLATINUM OFFICE LEASING PROGRAM?

Glossary of Common Leasing Terms

Above Standard Tenant Improvements: Improvements that exceed the building standard

Agent: One who acts for another as a fiduciary. A real estate license is required to act as an agent for another in real estate property transaction

Assignment: A transfer of an interest in real property, in this case, the leasehold interest.

Base Rent: An amount of rent before adding any escalations

Base Year: Usually the first year of a lease to which future operating expenses are compared for the purpose of calculating expense increase

Building Class: Class A normally post-1990 construction, Class B pre-1990 construction. Also used subjectively to describe the quality of a property. Class A excellent overall; Class B good overall; Class C older with some functional defects; Class D deteriorated needing renovations

Building Standard: The quality level of the materials the building is offering tenants for use in constructing the tenant improvements.

Build-out: The proposed construction for a new or renovated suite.

Capitalization Rate: The percentage rate applied to the net income to determine value. Also known as Cap Rate

Certificate of Occupancy: Issued by governing authorities certifying the right to occupy a property

Common Area: Building or project areas used in common with other tenants including service areas such as maintenance rooms, janitorial closets, etc.

Consumer Price Index: A governmental index used in determining the cost of goods and services. Use in leases to prevent the erosion of income by escalating the rent payable annually

Default: The failure to comply with an obligation required under the lease contract, may or may not be monetary

Demising Walls: The walls that separate one tenant from another or from the common areas

Effective Rent: The average of all the years of the rent after deducting any landlord concessions such as free rent or over standard tenant improvements

Estoppel Certificate: A certificate by tenant that the lease is full force and effect and confirming the economics of the lease

Expense Stop: Used to cap the amount the landlord is willing to pay to cover a particular expense or group of expenses such as operating expenses

First Right of Refusal: Grants a tenant the first right to match an offer to buy or lease a property or premises, or refuse such an offer after an offer has been tendered by a third party

Full Service Rent: An all inclusive rent covering rent, operating expenses, taxes and lessor's insurance, subject to escalations when these expenses increase after the first year of the lease

Hold Over Tenant: A tenant in possession after the lease term expiration

HVAC: Heating, Ventilating, and Air Conditioning Systems

Master Lease: The controlling lease covering a property, may control a subsequent lease or leases such as a sublease or assigned lease.

Mixed Use Project: More than one use within a project such as office and retail; office and hotel; office and apartments; retail and apartments

Mullions: Material used to divide window lines to allow for the attachment of walls in creating rooms.

Non-competition Clause: Prevents the owner from leasing space to another tenant that competes with an existing tenant.

Non-Disturbance: Protects a tenant from loss of its premises in the event of default by another party. If the owner is foreclosed, a non-disturbance agreement from the lender protects the tenant. If a sub-lessor defaults on a lease, non-disturbance agreement from the owner protects the sub-tenant

Notice of Lease Term Commencement: A document executed between owner and tenant defining the actual date the lease commenced, which may or may not define a new expiration date.

Parking Ratio: The number of parking spaces available per 1,000 square feet of space leased, or for an entire project

Pass-throughs: Operating expenses and/or tax increases paid by tenant under a lease agreement are said to be passed-through to tenant

Security Deposit: A deposit made by a tenant to a landlord to secure tenant's promise to perform its obligations under the lease

Space Plan: The preliminary space design defining the tenant's space requirements, often includes furniture layouts

Tenant Improvements: Improvements made to a property to make the space suitable for the tenant's intended use, whether paid for by landlord o tenant

Work-letter: A list of the quantity and type of component parts that will be used to construct tenant improvements, usually provided by landlord to secure a tenant for a property

Working Drawings: A complete set of plans, normally developed after lease execution, defining the precise layout and construction of the premises, suitable for obtaining permit and true costs

Zoning: A method used by government to regulate the use of property in a given area or zone. A set of ordinances controlling use.

SPACE NEEDS WORKSHEET

Items	Comments
Target Occupancy Date	
Preferred Geographic Location(s)	
Office Rent Budget Minimum Amount Maximum Amount	
Preferred Lease Term	
Site Accessibility Expressway Access Public Transportation	
Office Layout # of Cubicles/Offices	
Number of Employees	
Reception Area Size Seating Capacity	
Computer/Technology Requirements	
Work Areas/Mail Room # of Work Areas Storage Needs Equipment Requirements Special Electrical Needs	
Conference Rooms # of Rooms Seating Capacity Image Privacy	
Security	
Amenties Cafeteria Mail/Express Drop-offs Other Conveniences	
Parking Spaces Required Visitor Parking	
Image Building Office Space	

Office Space Rating Form						
Property Address:						
Suite Number:						
Quoted Rental Rate:						
Load Factor:						
Additional Expenses:						
	Notes	Rating				
		Excellent				Fair
Available Square Footage:		5	4	3	2	1
Reception Area:		5	4	3	2	1
# of Private Offices:		5	4	3	2	1
Amount of Open Area:		5	4	3	2	1
# of Conference Rooms:		5	4	3	2	1
Break Room:		5	4	3	2	1
Amount of Storage Space:		5	4	3	2	1
Computer/Tech Room:		5	4	3	2	1
Image:		5	4	3	2	1
Efficient Use of Space:		5	4	3	2	1
Location:		5	4	3	2	1
Opportunity for Expansion:		5	4	3	2	1

Office Space Rating Survey

Building 1	Excellent				Fair	Avg
Address:	5	4	3	2	1	
Available Square Footage						
Reception Area						
# of Private Offices						
Amount of Open Area						
# of Conference Rooms						
Break Room						
Amount of Storage Space						
Computer/Technology Room						
Image						
Efficient Use of Space						
Location						
Opportunity for Expansion						

Building 2	Excellent				Fair	
Address:	5	4	3	2	1	
Available Square Footage						
Reception Area						
# of Private Offices						
Amount of Open Area						
# of Conference Rooms						
Break Room						
Amount of Storage Space						
Computer/Technology Room						
Image						
Efficient Use of Space						
Location						
Opportunity for Expansion						

Summary:	Building 1	
	Building 2	

Proposal Evaluation

Proposal Items	Tenant's Request	Landlord's Response	Decision
Area/Square Footage			
Term			
Commencement Date			
Rental Rate			
Load Factor			
Operating Expenses			
Expansion Space			
Option to Extend			
Space Planning			
Tenant Improvements			
Assignment & Sublease			
Access			
Mechanical Systems			
Fire/Safety Systems			
Security			
Elevators			
Parking			
Building Ownership			
Property Management			
Amenities			
Standard Lease			
References			

Summary of Proposals

Proposal Items	Proposal 1	Proposal 2	Proposal 3
Area/Square Footage			
Term			
Commencement Date			
Rental Rate			
Load Factor			
Operating Expenses			
Expansion Space			
Option to Extend			
Space Planning			
Tenant Improvements			
Assignment & Sublease			
Access			
Mechanical Systems			
Fire/Safety Systems			
Security			
Elevators			
Parking			
Building Ownership			
Property Management			
Amenities			
Standard Lease			
References			

Lease Summary

Lease Term:	
Commencement Date:	
Expiration Date:	
Area:	

Rent Schedule	Start Date	Rate/Sq. Ft.	Monthly Rental

Security Deposit:	
Services Included:	
Operating Expense Allowance:	

Critical Lease Information

Date	Clause	Explanation

IMPORTANT BUILDING INFORMATION

Building Name:

Address:

Leasing Agent:

Agent's Phone Number:

Leasing Company:

Leasing Company Address:

Property Management Company:

Building Manager Contact:

Building Manager Phone Number:

Emergency/After-Hours Number:

Building Owner:

Owner's Mailing Address:

Other Important Information/Contacts:

MOVE-IN INSPECTION FORM

Center's name/address _____

Tenant's name _____

Parties present at inspection _____

Inspection date & time _____ Copy mailed to tenant on _____

1. EXTERIOR WALLS

▶ FRONT: ❏ Clean ❏ Graffiti ❏ Cracked

Comments _____

▶ REAR: ❏ Clean ❏ Graffiti ❏ Cracked

Comments _____

▶ LEFT SIDE: ❏ Clean ❏ Graffiti ❏ Cracked

Comments _____

▶ RIGHT SIDE: ❏ Clean ❏ Graffiti ❏ Cracked

Comments _____

2. INTERIOR WALLS

❏ Intact ❏ Major cracks ❏ Active leaks ❏ Leftover fixtures

Comments _____

3. SECURITY BARS ON WINDOWS

▶ FRONT: ❏ None ❏ Intact ❏ Broken

Comments _____

▶ REAR: ❏ None ❏ Intact ❏ Broken

Comments _____

▶ LEFT SIDE: ❏ None ❏ Intact ❏ Broken

Comments _____

▶ RIGHT SIDE: ❏ None ❏ Intact ❏ Broken

Comments _____

4. SECURITY DOOR/GATE

▶ FUNCTIONALITY: ❏ None ❏ Intact ❏ Broken

Comments _____

▶ APPEARANCE: ❏ Clean ❏ Graffiti

Comments _____

▶ LOCKING PIN(s): ❏ None ❏ Intact ❏ Broken

Comments _____

▶ PADLOCK PROVIDED BY _____

5. SIGNAGE

❏ None ❏ Intact ❏ Broken

Comments _____

6. ENTRANCE DOORS

▶ FRONT: ❏ None ❏ Intact ❏ Broken
Tenant has key(s): ❏ Yes ❏ No

Comments _____

▶ REAR: ❏ None ❏ Intact ❏ Broken
Tenant has key(s): ❏ Yes ❏ No

Comments _____

▶ LEFT SIDE: ❏ None ❏ Intact ❏ Broken
Tenant has key(s): ❏ Yes ❏ No

Comments _____

▶ RIGHT SIDE: ❏ None ❏ Intact ❏ Broken
Tenant has key(s): ❏ Yes ❏ No

Comments _____

7. INTERIOR DOORS/LOCKS

▶ DOORS: ❏ All intact # Broken _____

Comments _____

▶ LOCKS: ❏ All intact # Broken _____

Comments _____

8. WINDOWS

▶ FRONT: ❏ None Total # _____ ❏ All intact
# of cracked panels _____ # of missing panels _____
Weather stripping ❏ None # Cracked _____ # Missing _____

Comments _____

▶ REAR: ❏ None Total # _____ ❏ All intact
# of cracked panels _____ # of missing panels _____
Weather stripping ❏ None # Cracked _____ # Missing _____

Comments _____

▶ LEFT SIDE: ❏ None Total # _____ ❏ All intact
# of cracked panels _____ # of missing panels _____
Weather stripping ❏ None # Cracked _____ # Missing _____

Comments _____

► RIGHT SIDE: ❑ None Total # _____ ❑ All intact
_____ # of cracked panels _____ # of missing panels _____
Weather stripping ❑ None # Cracked _____ # Missing _____

Comments _____

9. SKYLIGHTS

► GLASS: ❑ None ❑ Intact # of cracked panels _____
# of missing panels _____

Comments _____

► SECURITY BARS: ❑ None ❑ Intact ❑ Broken

Comments _____

10. CEILING

❑ Intact # of missing panels _____ # of discolored panels _____

Comments _____

11. LIGHTING FIXTURES

of fluorescent fixtures _____ ❑ All intact # Broken _____
# of working bulbs _____ # of broken bulbs _____ # of missing bulbs _____
► SWITCHES: ❑ Intact ❑ Broken

Comments _____

12. FLOOR/CARPETING

► FLOOR TILES: ❑ Intact # of cracked tiles _____ # of loose tiles _____
► HARDWOOD FLOOR: ❑ Clean ❑ Scratched
► CARPETING: ❑ Clean ❑ Worn ❑ Torn ❑ Stained

Comments _____

13. BATHROOMS

MEN'S
► SINK: ❑ Functional ❑ Nonfunctional
► TOILET: ❑ Functional ❑ Nonfunctional
► TOWEL DISPENSER/HAND DRYER: ❑ Functional ❑ Nonfunctional

Comments _____

WOMEN'S
► SINK: ❑ Functional ❑ Nonfunctional
► TOILET: ❑ Functional ❑ Nonfunctional
► TOWEL DISPENSER/HAND DRYER: ❑ Functional ❑ Nonfunctional

Comments _____

14. UTILITY SINK

❑ None ❑ Functional ❑ Nonfunctional

Comments _____

15. HVAC

❑ Functional ❑ Nonfunctional # of working vents _____
# of nonworking vents _____

► THERMOSTATS: ❑ Functional ❑ Nonfunctional

Comments _____

16. AIR CONDITIONER UNITS/SPACE HEATERS

► SPACE HEATER: ❑ None Total # _____ ❑ Functional ❑ Nonfunctional
Properly installed and vented ❑ yes ❑ no

► AIR CONDITIONER UNITS: ❑ None Total # _____ ❑ Functional
❑ Nonfunctional Properly installed and vented ❑ yes ❑ no

Comments _____

17. METERS: GAS/ELECTRIC/WATER

► GAS METER: ❑ Functional ❑ Nonfunctional
Valve ❑ open ❑ closed ❑ locked

Acct. name _____

Last reading _____ Date _____

Comments _____

► ELECTRIC METER: ❑ Functional ❑ Nonfunctional
Service ❑ on ❑ off ❑ Meter locked

Acct. name _____

Last reading _____ Date _____

Comments _____

► WATER METER: ❑ Functional ❑ Nonfunctional Service ❑ on ❑ off

Acct. name _____

Last reading _____ Date _____

Comments _____

18. PHONE SYSTEM

❑ None ❑ Present Type _____ Model # _____
❑ Functional ❑ Nonfunctional
Comments _____

19. ALARM SYSTEM

❑ None ❑ Present Type _____ Model # _____
❑ Functional ❑ Nonfunctional Tenant has code ❑ yes ❑ no
Comments _____

Owner's/Manager's signature _____ Date _____

Tenant's signature _____ Date _____

FREE

Lease Proposal
Evaluation Consultation

($2,500 CONSULTATION VALUE)

This certificate entitles you to send a lease proposal with your specific question or business need. Robert will personally review and evaluate your proposal and you will receive a customized report including negotiating recommendations and current market data for your area.

Name: _____

Company: _____

Address: _____

City, State Zip: _____

Phone: _____

Fax: _____

Email: _____

Send to: **The Miller Group LLC**
P.O. Box 889274
Atlanta, GA 30356
Fax: 678-731-1575
www.tmgleasing.com

What is the Platinum Office Leasing Program?

The Platinum Office Leasing Program is an office space location and negotiation program designed specifically to support the needs and challenges of small to medium sized companies.

Most Platinum members are high level executives or the business owners either completely or partially responsible for the growth and long term strategic planning of their companies.

Your Platinum consultant meets with you and your key associates to study your business operations, space needs and company goals and objectives. Then designs a strategic plan to carefully guide you though the maze of real estate options...leasing... sale-lease-backs... investments... ownership structures... tax avoidance techniques... showing you the pros and cons of all choices.

If your business has over five employees with gross sales in excess of $1 million dollars and currently utilizes over 3,000 square feet of office space or conducts business using satellite locations you may be eligible for this elite program.

Call 770-451-4455 to find out if you qualify for this unique program.

NOTES

TreeNeutral

Advantage Media Group is proud to be a part of the Tree Neutral™ program. Tree Neutral offsets the number of trees consumed in the production and printing of this book by taking proactive steps such as planting trees in direct proportion to the number of trees used to print books. To learn more about Tree Neutral, please visit **www.treeneutral.com.** To learn more about Advantage Media Group's commitment to being a responsible steward of the environment, please visit **www.advantagefamily.com/green**

Negotiating Office Space is available in bulk quantities at special discounts for corporate, institutional, and educational purposes. To learn more about the special programs Advantage Media Group offers, please visit **www.KaizenUniversity.com or call 1.866.775.1696.**

Advantage Media Group is a leading publisher of business, motivation, and self-help authors. Do you have a manuscript or book idea that you would like to have considered for publication? Please visit **www.amgbook.com**

Printed in the USA
CPSIA information can be obtained
at www.ICGtesting.com
JSHW012034140824
68134JS00033B/3057